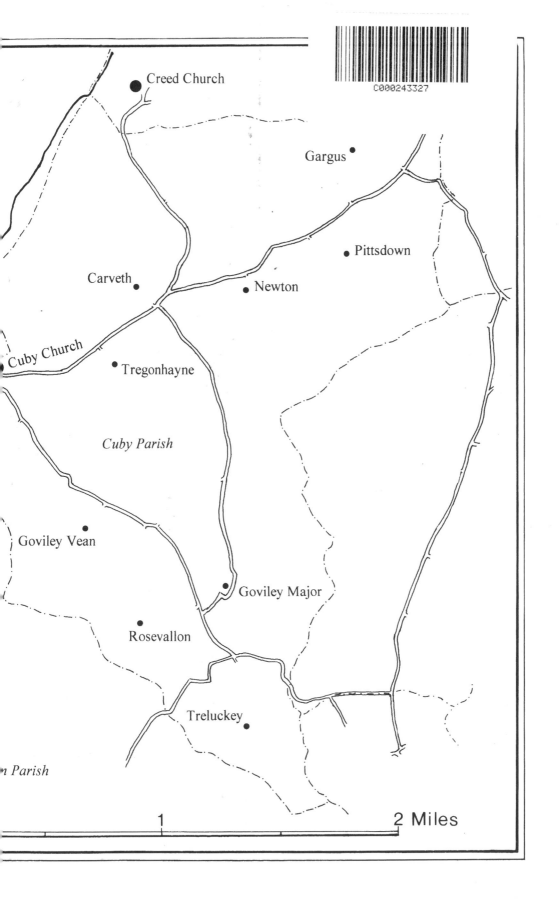

Creed Church

Gargus

Pittsdown

Carveth

Newton

Cuby Church

Tregonhayne

Cuby Parish

Goviley Vean

Goviley Major

Rosevallon

Treluckey

n Parish

1   2 Miles

TREGONY HAPPENINGS

TREGONY HAPPENINGS

Memories & Photographs of Tregony & District
1886~1921

Franklin Grigg

ISBN 0 9548912 0 1

First published in Great Britain in 2004
by
F. R. Grigg
Ymir, Tregrehan Mills,
St Austell,
Cornwall,
PL25 3TL

www.tregoneyhistory.co.uk

Printed by
Affordable Print Ltd,
Cornwall
01726 815842

Bound by
T. J. International Ltd,
Trecerus Industrial Estate,
Padstow, Cornwall
PL28 6RW

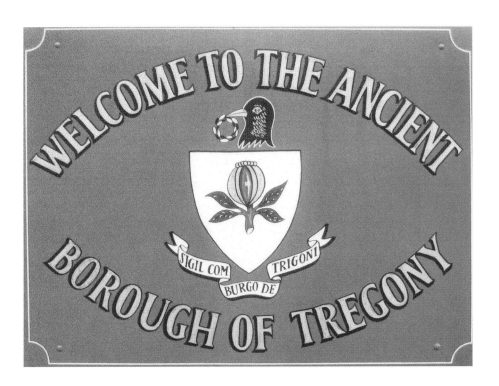

Contents

List of Illustrations

11

Acknowledgements

There are many people whose assistance has been essential in the compiling of this book. First and foremost I am indebted to Mrs Jessie Pollard and Mrs Pat Warne, relatives of the late Mr Frank Greet; and to the late Mrs Pauline Hooper, granddaughter of the deceased, Mr Joseph Greet, for giving me permission to use the writings and photographs, respectively, of these two gentlemen.

I am particularly grateful to the staff of the Cornwall Record Office, the Courtney Library at the Royal Institute of Cornwall and the Cornwall Centre at Redruth for all the assistance given and for permission to include copies of certain documents. I acknowledge with thanks the authority given by the following people and organisations to quote or reproduce certain items: Mr R. Vanhinsberg, Editor of the *West Briton*; Christine North; Mr Paul Rowling of Tregony Community Primary School; Tregony W.I.; The Commonwealth War Graves Commission; and The Order of the Oddfellows.

To the many generous people who have lent me photos and documents, I thank you. Especially to: Mrs P.Kendall-Carpenter for use of several of the photos in the collection of the late Mr David Kendall-Carpenter, the Peter Bray Collection, Mrs C.W. Kendall, Mr Pat Stapleton, Mr Roy Mountstephens, Mr Graham Blackler, Mr Peter Lidgey, Mr Robert Pollard, Mrs. H. Nicholls, Mr George Barnicoat, Mr William Barnicoat, Mr Richard Truscott, Mrs G. Hopkins, Mr & Mrs D.J.Stark, Mr Wilfred Lidgey, Mrs Rosa Blackler, Mr & Mrs Cliff Towsey, Mrs Karen Houser, Mrs Beard, Mrs M. Jones, Mr A. Nixon, Mr Gilbert Grigg, Mrs Bridget Best, Mr D.H. Tonkin, Mr Eric Chenoweth, Mrs Lorna Leadbetter, Mrs Joyce Sweatman, Miss J.L Roberts, Mrs A.I. Ince, Mr Russell Grose, Mrs Jean Biddick, Mr M.D.Grigg, Mr N. Penrose, Mr S. Richards, Mrs L. Bilkey, Mrs Pring, Mr Paul Henwood, Mr J. Nile, Mrs P.M. Burgess, the late Mr Kenneth Coad, the late Mrs Carrie Hocking, the late Mr George Miners, the late Mr Arthur Grigg, the late Mr Ronnie Spear, the late Mr Charlie Ford, the late Mrs Vera Hocking, the late Mrs Morval Jago, the late Mrs Mary Richards, the late Mr Mark Jacob, the late Mr Donald Mountstephens, the late Mrs M. Sadd, the late Mrs D. Lane, the late Mrs D. Rounsevell and the late Mrs Winnie Keast,

Personal thanks are also due to the many Tregonians who have patiently put up with my constant visits and questions. Their answers have assisted in the completion of this book: Mr & Mrs Martin Berryman, Mrs Joy Floyd-Norris, Mr Edgar Lidgey, Mrs Margaret Barnicoat, Mr Reg Greet, Mrs Jean Biddick, Mrs Rosa Blackler, Mr Graham Blackler, Mr Reg Matthews, the late Mr A. Lovell, Father Christopher Shepherd, Mr Norman Davey, Mr Pat Stapleton, Mr John Pascoe, Mr William H. Wheeler, Mr Dennis Curtis, Mr & Mrs Grayden Towsey, Mr & Mrs Cliff Towsey, Mr Maurice Beard, Mr Cecil Pearce, Mr Norman Pearce, Mrs A. Gibson, Mr Ian Greet, Mr David Roberts, Canon Michael Warner. To those whose names I may have unwittingly omitted, I apologise.

I wish to extend my sincere appreciation for the personal assistance given to me by Malcolm and Ann Trethowan, by Mike Ford and by Michael Williams.

A special tribute must be given to Mr Roger Penhallurick for the preparation of the wonderful maps included in the book. [Roger's untimely death occurred shortly after completing this work].

My final big thank you goes to my wife Sue, who has been my guide, inspiration and personal assistant for 'many a long hour'.

Introduction

The township of Tregony is located 17 miles from Falmouth and it is sited on the upper reaches of the River Fal. In past times the river was tidal up to and even beyond Tregony. The area has a very long and intriguing history which dates back to Norman times when the town was an inland port. In 1621 Tregony was granted a Charter of Incorporation which gave it a Free Borough status and this remained until 1849 when the Corporation ceased to exist.

Apart from several, locally distributed pamphlets and booklets, nothing has been published on the history of Tregony. My quest is to record the life in the district between 1886 and 1921.

The basis of "Tregony Happenings" has been compiled from the individual works of two local men, who, coincidentally, shared the surname of GREET. Whether they were related is uncertain.

- Mr Frank GREET (<u>1886</u>-1972). In the mid-1960s, he wrote and distributed two type-written booklets, called 'Tregony in the 80s' and 'All My Yesterdays'. Both recorded his early memories of everyday life in the village, especially schoolday remembrances. [**For easy identification, the written work of Mr Frank Greet has been reproduced here in bold print**].

- Mr Joseph GREET (1847-1923). In the period between the early 1890s and <u>1921</u>, he carried on his profession as a photographer. He lived in Tregony and he travelled throughout Cornwall.

Many of Joseph's original photographs can still be found in the village and this book's selection will complement Frank's written descriptions. To complete the picture I have included newspaper clippings along with my own research comments.

As many older Tregonians will remember, 'Tregony Happenings' was the name of a local news-sheet, published during the Second World War, which informed 'our boys' on active service of events back home. This book proudly bears the same name. Originally, the title was used in the 1920s to introduce a short, weekly column in the *Royal Cornwall Gazette*, reflecting Tregony news events, in verse form.

Tregony or Tregoney? There has been a great debate over the years as to which is correct. The answer is both spellings are correct. However, 'Tregony' is now preferred. In the 1920s, newspaper reports often used both versions in the same article.

Franklin Grigg   September 2004
                                                              St Austell

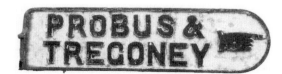

A Brief Biography of Mr Joseph GREET
the photographer

Joseph Truscott GREET was not a professional photographer until he was about 47 years old. Earlier, his working life was mostly spent on the land and in the mining industry.

He was born in the Parish of Cuby (Tregony) on the 9th May 1847 to local agricultural stock. The 1861 Census reveals that the Greet family had moved to the mining district of Lanner Moor (Redruth). Joseph gained mining skills and, like many miners of this era, he travelled overseas in search of work. From the USA he returned to become a Captain in one of the small, Welsh, gold-mines.

By 1891, Joseph was married with four daughters, and a mining accident forced a career change. The family moved to Tregony and Joseph the photographer was established. It is probable that his initial enthusiasm for photography was kindled whilst

working in the USA. His 'photographic and picture framing' business flourished until about 1921. He worked at his trade taking portraits and recording events and places. In a pony and trap, he travelled mainly throughout Mid-Cornwall and the Roseland areas fulfilling his photographic contracts. Often his 'conveyance' could be seen discreetly visible in the background of many of his shots.

He did not become widely well-known but, locally, his work was well regarded and his services much sought after. Many of his photographs still remain and they show a wonderful insight into the feelings of the day. He turned many of his pictures into postcards, but for some reason he never endorsed his name on them. His photographic prints were always embossed with his own trade stamps. If you ever see an old photo of Tregony, have a look at the back, it is probably one of Joseph Greet's.

Mr Greet died at Tregony on the 30th October 1923 and he is buried in the church cemetery.

A Brief Biography of Mr Frank GREET
the storyteller

Francis Mountstephen GREET was a Tregony man, born on the 4th February 1886, the fifth child of James and Mary Greet. He attended Tregony Board School until the age of 12 and then left to work for a local horse-bus proprietor, named Caleb Greet. (By coincidence, Caleb was a brother to Joseph Greet, the photographer.)

He was orphaned in 1901 when his widowed mother died and he moved to Penzance to become a stable boy with a local vet. It was whilst in Penzance that he caught, what he described as, the 'Navy fever', i.e. his zest to "see the world". In 1902 Frank joined the Royal Navy. After receiving a very harsh training he went to sea, but by 1905, his Navy days were over; he was discharged because of an eye complaint.

Frank returned to Tregony with a much greater insight into life and a strong empathy for his fellow workers. He found employment in the mines and clayworks around St Austell. In 1909 he married and moved to the St Dennis area where he became an Independent Labour Party Member. He joined the Trade Union movement and in 1913 was one of the leaders in the St Austell Clay Strike. In 1970 he took part in a BBC television documentary entitled, 'The White Country', which re-enacted the strike.

After the First World War, Frank and his family returned to Tregony, where he set up business, initially as a deliveryman selling his own vegetables and then as a shopkeeper in the 'Central Stores'. It was from then that he was able to take a real interest in the social and political life of Tregony. His boundless energy and his great sense of public spiritedness were both put to good use in the planning, fundraising and running of all the many organisations and committees in which he became involved: Truro RDC, the Parish Council, Feast Committee, British Empire Cancer Foundation and the Workers' Educational Association, just to name a few.

Mr Greet was responsible for producing the 'Tregoney Happenings' news-sheets (1943-1945) during the Second World War. In the 1960s, for the benefit of later generations, he wrote down his recollections of life in Tregony during his younger days.

He died at Tregony on the 10th May 1972, aged 86, and he is buried in the local cemetery.

LET THE MYSTERY BE !

In the 1930s, Frank Greet built a new family bungalow (Hart Lea) on the site of the old Hart House School. Typically displaying his futuristic approach to life, he implanted a 'time capsule' into the wall of his bungalow. Items of the 1930s were included, yet, more importantly, he encased relics recovered from Doctor Hart's School. The box is still *in situ*.

Chapter 1

THE BEGINNING

I am writing my memoirs of Tregony in the 1890s, as I saw it and how the people lived and worked and what the Village looked like. It is written chiefly for Tregonians present and future, as no doubt they will be reminded of some of the stories they have been told.

Tregony Football Team 1903-4.
(back row, l -r) R.J.Real, George Dowrick, Sgt Kendall, Peter Burley, George Towsey, Arthur Nicholls, Matthew Blackler, Epplet Roberts.
(mid row) Fred Roberts, u/k, Jack Beard, Edward C. Barnicoat.
(front) Moses Barnicoat, Mark Jacob, u/k, Willie Barnicoat.

To begin – we must look back a little to the time when Tregony was a Borough Town. In fact, in my boyhood days, we always talked of Tregony as a 'Town', such as Top Town and Bottom Town. We had the Town Clock (with one hand), a Town Band, a Town Oven, a Town Crier, a Town Lamplighter, a Town Football Team and of course a Town Arms, which is still licensed. Also a Town

Market Place behind the Town Clock. Tregony's connection with by-gone days is an interesting one. Between 1295 and 1307, Tregony had sent only four Members to Parliament, the custom had then lapsed. In 1562, Queen Elizabeth 1st recreated the Borough of Tregony by Royal Decree and between 1562 and 1832 Tregony elected 148 Members to Parliament. Tregony was no ordinary Borough; it was known as a 'Potwalloper Borough', where the vote was given to the Freemen. A Freeman was a man who could prove he provided his own food, was master of his fireplace at which he could cook and that he was in control of a doorway leading to his dwelling. Eating a meal in public occasionally was a gesture by the Freemen to prove themselves free and self-sustained, eating not the bread of servitude nor owing fealty to any overlord. This custom of having a meal in the Fore Street is still observed on all great national days, such as Coronation, Jubilee and Peace celebrations, etc., so let one and all who take part in these events, spare a passing thought for those who began this custom some 300 years before.

Tregony Bridge - late 1890s. Completed in 1893, it replaced an older version. The gent, 3rd from the right is Mr May

I have already mentioned that this story is written mainly for relatives and friends and those who may have some interest in Tregony. It is briefly told of the years 1892 to 1901, which comprised my schooldays, after which I was away for a few years.

I was born in 1886, the fifth child of James and Mary Greet at Castle View, Tregony which at that time was the biggest thatched cottage of Swine Street, (afterwards renamed Well Street), and which was situated on what is now the garden below the Square, by Well Street. My first memory was the famous blizzard of 1891, which left all roads impassable till the County's able-bodied men had worked many weeks to clear them. I attended the Tregony Board School, until the age of 12 when I left to commence work for Mr Caleb Greet, a bus proprietor, who also kept cows and pigs, as well as five horses. My wages commenced at 3/6d per week, which may seem small, but was the average for small boys at the time.

My memories – I remember the old Tregony Bridge being rebuilt and widened in about 1893, and the first telegraphy poles being erected in Tregony. Also passing two blacksmiths on the hill, each working two smiths; the old Brianite Chapel where Billy Bray had preached. Of the 'Gallery', I recall seeing only the walls and chimneys standing prior to its restoration in 1895.

At Frogmore, Dr Bennett kept two horses, a coachman and two servant girls. In Edie's Court was the old Malt House Yard. All three Inns, including the Gregor Arms at the far end of Tregony Bridge, brewed their own ale. Across the Square, in Pig Street (now Well Street), was the Town Oven and the shop-come Post Office, 'open 8 till 8', delivering and collecting once every day.

Just below Gurney Row was the Police lock-up. On the opposite side of Fore Street was Agar Hop, leading through where the fish and chip shop is now. There was also Yarmouth Row of two or three poor houses, and up beyond the Town Clock, the Rectory (now the antique shop) where the Rector held a 'Blanket Club' (a form of friendly society). On the site of the present Village Hall stood twelve back-to-back houses. Just above that was the boot-maker's shop, the thatched houses of Coronation Terrace and beyond that again, Dobel Lane. There was also Cox's Row of six cottages, let at 1/- a week. What is now Pine Cottage was the Hart House School's tuck shop and on the opposite side at No. 41 Fore Street, the School's isolation infirmary and with the stables downstairs.

Tregony, as everyone knows, is now an agricultural village, known as the 'Gateway to the Roseland', but in former days, it was a market town and noted for its industries, such as wool combing, clock making, boot making, monumental masons and many other various trades, but these have now ceased to exist.

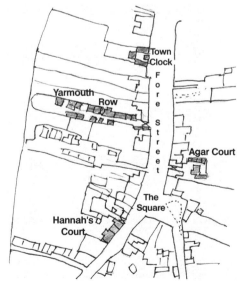

A sketch plan of lower Fore Street, Tregony showing the site names of places that have since disappeared. The Author 2004

Additional Information

Tregony's Vanished Street Names
The majority of the land and houses within the old Tregony Borough were owned by a few wealthy and influential landowners

who resided elsewhere. Many small houses, some constructed with just 'one up and one down rooms', were built by the Barons and let cheaply to the labouring classes. However, occupancy came with implied conditions and the Master's wishes were sacrosanct, especially where voting in national elections was concerned. These landowners were frequently the backers for

Hannah's Court was situated somewhere between the archway to Eadie's Court and the 3rd house down (Mrs Barnicoat's). The Author 2004

The entrance to Yarmouth Row. Access was gained to the cul-de-sac via the archway which is located about 40 yards up from Gurney Row. The Author 2004

The remnants of Yarmouth Row. A 1991 photo taken from inside the Row and looking out towards Fore Street. The walls of abandoned houses can be seen on both sides of the Row.
The Author

the prospective Members of Parliament and they 'demanded' their tenants must vote according to the landowner's wishes. A tenant's complicity was expected when a 'no vote, no house' policy could reveal opposing tenants whose cast vote was not confidential.

In 1832, Tregony, having been deemed a 'Rotten Borough' was disenfranchised as a Parliamentary Constituency. As power had been taken from the area, the wealthy landowners left and the value of property diminished. Much of the old-type housing remained, but gradually, because of lack of maintenance, the premises were demolished. A few such addresses that have disappeared in Tregony are cited below. Most of these dwellings were constructed between the 1790s and the 1830s.

Hannah's Court. *(Formerly Luke's Court).* This was a row of three houses that was located somewhere between Eadies Court and Frogmore House, in the area known today as 23 to 25, Tregony Hill. In the 1881 Census, two houses were listed in Luke's Court. Between 1891 and 1901 its name became Hannah's Court.

Yarmouth Row. *Remnants of this long cul-de-sac are apparent in the centre of Tregony, about 40 yards up from Gurney Row. Access is gained by an archway off Fore Street. Small terraced houses used to line both sides of this narrow row. In 1841, 12 houses were occupied, but at the time of the 1901 Census, only five houses remained. The occupancy of the last of the inner-sited dwellings ceased in the late 1920s. Since then these buildings have collapsed with decay. One dwelling is still occupied, and this is located just inside the entrance.*

Agar Court. *Named after the Agar Family who were landowners in the Borough in the early 1800s. This little-known court, which is still located on the opposite side of Fore Street, to Gurney Row, is accessed via an arched opening. The records showed three or four occupied houses between 1881 and 1901.*

Chapel Terrace. *(Also previously known as Lower Well Row or Giggen Row). This consisted of twelve small, back-to-back houses built on the site where the Village Hall now stands. These abodes provided shelter until about 1946/7, when they were demolished for the first Hall to be erected.*

Coronation Terrace. *(Previously named Corporation Row and, prior to that, Higher Well Row). The terrace*

Agar Court - 2004. The entrance to the small Court is via the archway. The author

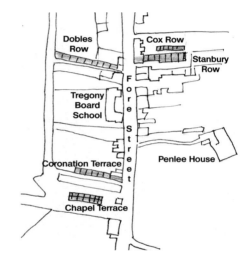

A sketch plan of higher Fore Street, Tregony, showing the locations of the places that have disappeared. The Author 2004

A 1930s snapshot of part of Chapel Terrace which once stood on the site where the Village Hall presently stands. Unknown source

Coronation Terrace, Tregony - 1996. Located off Fore Street some 30 yards up from the Village Hall. Only two houses now remain. The Author

Dobles Row or Ope, Tregony. Situated just above the old Village School, this narrow thoroughfare joins Fore Street to Back Lane. The Author 2004

Cox or Cock's Row, Tregony. The entrance to this ancient Row was via the lane located between the bungalow and the telephone pole. The Author 2004

still exists, yet only two houses remain. It is situated just off Fore Street and to the north of the Village Hall. An 1828 map showed eight houses. By 1901, seven houses were listed. Most of the Row was condemned and demolished by 1957.

Dobles Row. This small lane survives just above the old Tregony County Primary School, and connects Fore Street to Back Lane. The last houses recorded there, were in 1881 when three were counted. An earlier 1828 map showed at least ten houses lining both side of this Row. About twenty years ago a garage was erected at the 'Back Lane' end of this row, and since, the route has deviated around the building.

Cock's or Cox Row. This block of six small, terraced houses was sited at the top part of Fore Street, on the opposite side of the road to the present 'Memorial, Children's Play Park'. The Row was accessed via a small lane. The dwellings were condemned and demolished in about 1947.

Stanbury Row. This terrace, which is located just above Penlee Close, although still in existence, is much altered from its original appearance. Only two properties now remain. The 1841 Census showed 15 families residing in the Row. By 1901 there were seven houses still standing and this number remained until most of the Row was knocked down in about 1957.

Conce Lane. To most of the older generation of Tregonians, even today, this unclassified road, which leads from just below the Parish Church out towards Cuby Close, is known as Conce Lane. In recent times it has been renamed Cuby Lane.

Stanbury Row, Tregony, located approx 20 yards up from Penlee Close. Most of the houses were demolished in 1957. The Author 2004

Melbourne House. At the beginning of the 1900s, a detached house was built on a large plot of land located 100 yards down from the Parish Church on the right-hand side of Fore Street. It was known as Melbourne House. The owner was a local thatcher, Alfred Davey. The dwelling remained occupied until 1992 and three years later it was demolished for the construction of two modern detached houses. They are named Melbourne Cottage and Melbourne House. This site has a history of ownership. In 1829 a Town School was erected there. It was run on the 'British System' and it was built to accommodate 300 children. (This school predated the Village Board School which opened in 1877.)

A 1992 photo of the original Melbourne House. The Author

Much of the original school building remained when Mr Davey erected his house. He incorporated one of the old walls into the structure of the back kitchen.

Melbourne Cottage & Melbourne House. These two modern houses were built on the site of the original Melbourne House. The Author 2004

Mr Norman Davey, a grandson of Alfred, recently related a story which involved his grandfather using an 'old ways' method of pinpointing an ancient well which had been con-

The original Tregony Post Office & Stores. The 'X' marks the two properties in which the old P.O. & stores were housed. N.B. Lidgey's Garage had just been sold for development. The Author December 1997

cealed within the garden. Apparently he planted the whole area with seed potatoes. The site of the well was eventually identified by the circular patch of underdeveloped potatoes because the moisture in the soil had drained, thus restricting growth. (Possibly, water divining had not been successful).

Further history came to light after checking the original property deeds. In 1864, this parcel of land was purchased on behalf of the Justices of the Peace for Cornwall to construct a Cornwall Constabulary Police Station. However, the plans never materialised and a house opposite The Square continued to be used by the Police.

The Village Post Office Location. The 1880 Ordnance Survey Map confirmed Mr Frank Greet's account that the Post Office, at that time, was located in Fore Street, immediately above The Square. The shop occupied a large building which now equates to the present adjoining addresses of 1, The Square and 1 Fore Street. The postmaster was James Stephens who with his wife and daughter operated a grocery business and post office since at least 1873. The family continued as proprietors until about 1897.

Soon afterwards, the new Postmaster, Mr Richard Truscott, together with his family,

opened the next branch at the present site, at 10a Fore Street (on the opposite side of the road to the clock tower). The Truscott family retained the business until 1967, when Mr Grenville Truscott (son) retired. This Post Office is still open for business at the same address.

The present Tregony Post Office. This is a 1905 photo of the Truscott family who ran the present P.O. from 1897 to 1967.
(l-r) Mr Richard Truscott (postmaster); Richard Grenville Truscott (son); Cyril J. Truscott (son); Winnifred J. Truscott (dau); Mrs Grace Truscott (wife) & Emma G. Truscott (dau).

Chapter 2

THE TRADESMEN & BUSINESSES

In trying to record a list of tradesmen and businesses, it is a little difficult to point out to readers where they were situated, but after looking through Kelly's record of Tregony and its people and their occupations, etc, I think I will do it likewise.

GROCERS SHOPS
Mrs Beard
Miss M.G. Bennett
Mrs M.A. Thomas
Mrs J. Willcock
Mr J. Holyoake
Mrs A. Strongman
Mr N. Coombe
Mr S. Tregenza
Miss R. Banfield
Mrs Roberts
Mr J. Stephens
Mrs R. Tonkin
Mr H.E. Roberts

DRAPERS
Mr J. Tregunna
Mr A.J. Harris

PACKMEN
Mr M. Mills
Mr S.J. Lidgey
Mr J. Woolcocks

CARPENTERS
T. Harris & Sons
W. Gerrans & Sons
Stephen Bennett
C. Beard
F. Hicks
J. Barnicoat
W. Barnicoat
J.M. Carkeek
N. Carkeek
R.H. Tonkins (builders & contractors)

SHOEING & GENERAL SMITHS
Mr R. Barnicoat
T. Barnicoat
J. Barnicoat
H.E. Roberts
J. Holyoake
I. Grose
J. Jacob

MASONS
S. Mountstephen & Sons
F. Tonkin
J. Tonkin
A. Bennetts
W. Evans
G. Towsey (senior)
G. Towsey (junior)

SHOEMAKER
D. Barnicoat

SADDLERS
A. Chenoweth
J. Nicholls

COBBLERS
H. Jacob

RABBIT TRAPPERS
F. Burley
W. Keast

THATCHERS
Alfred Joseph Boswell
George Davy

PROFESSIONAL
Dr. Bennett

VETERINARY SURGEON
G. Channon

EXCISE OFFICER
Mr Leslie

PLUMBER
T. Dowrick

HARWARE & CHINA
J. Hicks
E. Cox

POTATO MERCHANTS
J. Harris
G. Grose
W.H. Nicholls
R. Miners
J. Willcocks
J. Greet

BUTCHERS
J. Furze
W.Dowrick (pork butcher)

POLICE
Sergeant Davis
Constable Cook

CARTERS
J. Truscott
G. Miners
D. Barnicoat
J. May

TOWN CRIER
Horsea Snell

BUS & CARRIAGE PROPRIETORS
Caleb Greet
Joseph Tonkin

FLY PROPRIETORS
W.J. Roberts
J. Tonkin (junior)

HABERDASHERY
T. Tiller
J. Catermole

PHOTOGRAPHER
Joseph Greet

PUBS
King's Arms – J. Davey
Town Arms –
    Misses Elliott
Gregor Arms – J. Evans

COAL MERCHANTS
F. Cox
A. Beard

*Tregony approx 1895. Mr Alfred Davey and son, Herbert, thatching the roof of Penlee Cottage.
Brewer's waggon of Grampound Road is delivering the straw for the thatch.*

From a 1904 postcard – The parade passes the Bennett sisters' grocery/bakers shop, situated by the entrance to Stanbury Row.

Tregony circa 1900. Mr George Channon, the local vet, with his mother Mrs Jane Channon and sister, Miss Mary Ann Channon. In the background is their house, Glenview, Fore Street.

In completing this list, it seems to me that there were not many more people left. In fact, there was almost every kind of shop, except a pawnshop. The rea-

A group of Tregony masons photographed in the late 1890s. (Back row, l-r) - George Towsey (sen); Aaron Barnicoat; --Dowrick; William Pearce? (front row) Bob Lyndon; Will Keast; u/k; George Towsey (jun).

son for that I think was, that the better off people had no reason to pawn, and the poor had nothing to pawn, except their faces, which they often did to the tradesmen; but of course, good tradesmen were very sympathetic and the bailiffs were not around often.

After reading the list of all these trades-

people, you may wonder how they all got their living. The reason was, I think, because Truro and St Austell would be a long way off in those days with only horse transport to and fro. The 1/- return fare meant quite a bit out of a man's wages of 2/6d, so the little shops used to provide for most of the villagers and the surrounding country cottages. The population then would be about 500 at least. I know it was just under that in the next census.

It is not necessary to point out how each trade managed, but I will mention

Pasty time for the lady potato pickers of Tregony. This photo was taken during the First World War.

just a few. First, the largest General Store was run by Mr J. Stephens, which included the Post Office. The others were all of the nature of a village grocery but as there were no prepared foods (or very little in those days) the stock they carried was the main articles of food.

The two carpenters, Messrs W. Gerrans and T. Harris, were also wheelwrights and undertakers which greatly enhanced their business. Most of the masonry work for the village was done by S. Mountstephens and other journeymen.

There were three full-time blacksmiths and shoeing shops each with apprentices, but today there is none. To have a horse shod now, one has to travel miles. One man, who was an apprentice then with Mr R. Barnicoat, namely Mr Eddy Grose, and is now retired, tells me that they worked

Chenoweth's Saddlers Shop, Tregony approx 1892. (Adjoining Myrtle House).
(l-r) Netta Chenoweth (dau); Arthur Chenoweth (saddler); u/k man; Mrs Charlotte Chenoweth (wife).

Saddler Chenoweth and his wife outside their shop in Fore Street. Details of the travellers are unknown.

from 8 a.m. to 8 p.m. because horses to be shod and other work would be brought in after 5 p.m. to be ready for the morning. The shoeing prices were:

Donkeys & Ponies – 1/6d per set;
Cobs – 1/8d and
Heavy Horses – up to 2/6d per set.

No wonder the smiths' brows were wet with honest sweat and it would be a joyful sound today to hear again the ring of the anvil and the bellows' roar; also to smell the smoke from the hoof.

There was one saddler, a Mr A. Chenoweth with a journeyman and apprentice full-time, but today not one.

Our plumber, Mr Thomas Dowrick, was a good tinsmith; besides doing any necessary plumbing, he made all the buckets, strainers and milk churns for the farmers throughout the Roseland.

The photographer, Mr Joseph Greet, will be remembered for many a year by his photos of persons and groups throughout a wide area. During his travels he took many photographs of rural scenes etc and I think I can say there is hardly a cottage which does not contain at least one of his photographs.

The potato merchants mentioned attended Truro on Saturdays. It may seem strange that so many went from Tregony, but in those days, grocers did not sell potatoes and most people depended on the potato carts when they bought their supply for a week; of course there were many other potato carts from other districts too, supplying Tregony.

Tregony approx 1909. A group of local men 'rinding' (removing bark from trees as a source of tannin for the leather tanning industry) in Colick Wood, Cornelly. (l-r) Fred Dowrick; George Towsey; Charlie Towsey; Lew Burley; Tom Towsey; Dick Blight; Will Keast. The young boy is Sam Dowrick.

The Slingers

In the foregoing list, I think it is plain to see that although agriculture was the main industry, not many agricultural workers lived in Tregony, except of course the 'Slingers', who were many; most of the tradesmen were journeymen, some of course working on the estates of Trewarthenick and Trewithen. As most farms had their workers' cottages, not many regular farm hands went out from Tregony. The regular farm hands and the char-ladies too, who used to go out to work, deserve our thanks because their names were never written in the Directory, but as my Uncle Bill used to say, that the farm workers and the farmers of course were the backbone of England, and he also said that they were the only indispensable men in the world. He often sang the 'Ploughboy's Song', one verse of which was as follows:

"Now all you jolly tradesmen
You feel so very grand
You say that your trades
Will support all the land,
But should the plough just stand still
For a very little while
All you jolly tradesmen
Will soon cease to smile."

Slingers was a term used for men who did the casual work, most of them were qualified to do almost any job on a farm, many of them were specialists in certain jobs, such as stone-hedging, sheep-shearing, quarrying, rinding

Tregony postcard 1909. Sinking a bore hole on the moors across the road from the Gregor Arms, Cornelly. Written on the card was, 'this is the mine at Tregony.' (Back row, l-r) – Fred Dowrick; George Towsey (jun); Lewis Burley. (Front row) -- Julyan?; Mr Gregory (in charge); Charlie Towsey & George Towsey (sen).

oak poles, thatching, wood-cutting and many other jobs, mostly done by piece-work. After harvest time, most of their work was threshing, for which they got 6d or 1/- per day extra. Most of the slingers kept a dog, a greyhound or lurcher, which could pick up a rabbit, and of course they kept ferrets and nets. Some knew how to set a wire, which enabled them to buy the rabbits of a farm, so in their spare time they went rabbiting. There were plenty of rabbits in those days and a hare occasionally; the price of a rabbit would be 6d to 8d each and hares quite a few shillings, 5/- to 6/- I think.

Regarding the slingers who went threshing during the season, they were often allowed a 'perk', such as a bundle of straw, and very often they would bring it for miles to sell it to some villager, who kept a cow or donkey, for 6d. The bundles were always hand-bound. It took four men to bind the straw from the threshing machine, with thumb beams. A beam or binding was made with a bit of straw woven around the thumb until it was about 5 feet in length to take a large bundle. In about 1895, a trusser was invented to bind with string; the trusser at that time being separate and built on two wheels with shafts for a horse to draw it from place to place, where it was connected to the machine. This trusser was soon replaced by another which was attached and of course it made threshing simpler. This latest type is in use today, where the threshing machine is still used.

An 1890s bill heading for Thomson Brothers of Tregony. CRO (AD591/3)

The Hinds

The men who lived in the rent-free farm cottages (known as hinds) had free

A threshing machine in action at Carveth Farm, Cuby in about 1918. The old gent (arm sling) is William May (sen).

Tregony Threshing Society – late 1920s. This Burrell engine was built in 1919. It was later owned by the Tregony Co-operative. In this picture it is being used for stone crushing at Treworgan Quarry near Ladock.

potato ground, milk and faggot wood for the cutting and some farms gave little bonuses such as 1/- per head for all fat cattle sold and 3d per lamb. One farm I knew provided a fat pig killed to his workmen once a year at about 2d per lb. (*pound weight*) which would be half the butcher's price. With these 'perks' and rabbits for the catching, it explained how a farm worker with a family lived on low wages. His pay in Cornwall was above many other counties, save the Northern industrial districts where it was much higher; the reason for this being that Cornwall had so many mines, clayworks and fishing to take a large proportion of workers.

Building the Grigg family haystack at Pitts Downs Farm, Cuby in approx 1910.

There were eight regular men from the Village who worked at Tregonhayne in addition to six who lived in their cottages as hinds. The Thomson Brothers also farmed Carveth, Barwick, Furda Downs and carried on a large forage and seed business, besides two portable steam threshing sets, which they let out to other farmers. These threshing sets were drawn from farm to farm by horses – four for the engine and four for the machine. During the summer season the firm employed quite a number of extra men as slingers.

Trewarthenick Estate employed eight men – a carpenter, four woodsmen and three odd job men as well as a keeper, gardeners and stablemen. The Trewithen Estate (Probus) employed a carpenter, a blacksmith, each with an apprentice.

Roadmen

The regular number employed on the roads by the Rural District Council was four and each man had several miles to look after at 15/- per week, but hedge pruning in the summer was done by contract at so much per mile.

Additional Information

Some of the forgotten skills of our agricultural 'craftsmen' can be seen in an article in the Royal Cornwall Gazette on the 16 October 1913, when the results were given of a demonstration and contest held at Ruanhighlanes. (Note the terms used to describe the events.)

Agricultural demonstrations were given on Thursday under the auspices of the Roseland Division of Cornwall County Council. Results:-
Ploughing
Turnwrest Plough Open – 1st C. Sleeman (Kenwyn). 2nd T. Hicks (Cuby).
Digge Turnwrest Plough – winners from Veryan and St Just.
Single Turnwrest Plough – 1st H. Freethy (Cuby).
Any Kind Turnwrest Plough under 18 – 1st E. Tregunna (Veryan).

Hedging
Stone Open – 2nd W.H. Julyan (Tregoney).
Jack & Joan Work – 1st G. Dowrick (Tregoney), 2nd S. Davey (Veryan), 3rd G. Lidgey (Tregoney).
Jack & Joan, (over 21 who have never won 1st prize) – S. Ford (Tregoney).
Upright Work (men over 21) – The winners were from Veryan.
Casting & Rising Hedge – 3rd W. Keast (Tregoney).

Horse Shoeing
Men under 21 – 1st J.H. Chenoweth (Tregoney).

Royal Cornwall Gazette – 12th October 1921 – Skilful Ploughmen

'Gratification is felt, writes a Tregoney correspondent, at the fact that several prizes came into

our Tregoney District from the Agricultural Demonstration at Tregoose on Saturday last. Our labourers have always excelled in all branches and are constantly well represented in the prize lists. We note that one of the best workmen, Mr George Dowrick of Tregoney, was selected as one of the judges of the thatching. Mr Matthew Blackler won the first prize in thatching and his elder brother, Charles, now residing at Trelowth, won the second prize. Our old friend, Mr W.H. Keast, also figured in the thatching prize list'.

This 1920s photo shows the blacksmith's shop at the bottom of Tregony Hill (right foreground). The open ground opposite, was also utilised by the smith.

A 1996 view looking down Tregony Hill onto the old smithy. It was later demolished and a dwelling was built on the site. The Author

Blacksmiths' Shops

Mr Frank Greet has already mentioned the blacksmiths who worked in Tregony, so before memories completely fade, it is worth noting the locations of the three main blacksmiths' shops in the Village at the turn of the 20th Century. All three 'smithies' were known to have been in existence in the 1880s and it is probable that they hold a more ancient history.

1. **Tregony Hill**. *This small, single-storied, cob building was located at*

Grand View, Tregony Hill. It was here in the front garden that another blacksmith's shop was located. It was last used in the 1930s and has long since disappeared. The Author 2004

the bottom of Tregony Hill on the right-hand side (i.e. when leading into the Village). The structure was demolished in 1997 and a house, named 'The Old Blacksmith Shop', was erected on the site. The last blacksmith to have worked there was believed to have been Mr Wilfred Dowrick, who finished in 1957. Afterwards, the premises became a car repair shop.

2. **Tregony Hill.** This was the second 'shop' in the Hill, and was situated on the right-hand side, just above the junction with Well Lane, in the front garden of the house now called 'Grand View'. All semblances of the building have disappeared. The 'smithy' was probably last used in the 1930s and it was associated with the Roberts family who had a long tradition in the profession.

3. **Gerrans Ope.** (Now known as Penlee Close). Entering the cul-de-sac, the original sheds were located in the far left-hand corner. A carpenter and a blacksmith worked side by side in adjoining 'shops'. Today, nothing remains of the establishments and modern bungalows have replaced them. The last of the 'smiths' to use this site was believed to have been Mr Cecil Miners in the early 1960s. (He was also the Church organist for many years). Previously, one of Tregony's most respected blacksmiths, Mr Eddy Grose, was in situ for many years. The carpenter who shared the site was Mr Gerrans. The Ope's name is in recognition of his family, who were much respected local builders and carpenters. In the 1930s, Mr Dunstone took over the carpenters shop.

Gerrans Ope, Tregony – early 1900s. (now known as Penlee Close). The site of the adjoining carpenter's and blacksmith's shops. Mr Gerrans (carpenter), worked in the left-hand shed and the blacksmith operated next door.

Chapter 3

TRANSPORT

The only transport was by horse-drawn vehicles, such as buses, wagonettes or two-wheeled dog-carts. There were also two 'fly proprietors' who owned dog-carts drawn by a pony. Strange as it may seem, I did not know myself what a 'fly proprietor' was until recently, when looking at a diary.

First, the bus services. There were two buses to Truro on Mondays, Wednesdays and Saturdays and one on Thursdays. Naturally it was only one trip leaving Tregony – one at 9 a.m. and the other at 11 a.m. and returning about 7.30 p.m. giving the customer four or five hours in town. The fare was 1/- return, but besides passengers, lots of parcels were carried at 2d or 3d carriage, also quite a bit of general cargo, such as timber, rods of iron for the smiths and, in general, anything that could be lifted on to the top of the bus. All buses had to come by way of Freewater Hill and Dabbs Hill, where all passengers had to get out and walk, which was quite reasonable with the load carried. Elderly or sick were allowed to remain by request, but very often there would be a grumble by some who thought they had a right to ride as well, but Caleb decided the issue.

It was my job on Wednesdays and Saturdays evenings to meet the bus with a third horse which was unhitched at the top of the hill and hitched up again at Tregony Hill, and the same business was done by Mr Tonkin. Both these proprietors kept smaller vehicles for wed-

Late 1890s. This damaged photo shows Caleb Greet's horse-bus named, 'The Telephone' stationary at the top of Tregony Hill.

Elliott's Town Arms, Tregony circa 1905. Absalom Beard, the carriage driver with guests from the hotel. The lady in the white dress is one of the Elliott sisters.

A postcard dated 1904. The occupants of the car are thought to have been members of the Tangey family from Newquay. A crowd gathers outside of Bennetts's shop.

dings and other hire work. Buses had their names in large coloured lettering on each side – Mr Greet's was 'The Telephone' and Mr Tonkin's 'The Albion'. In fact all the buses plying to Truro had their names such as 'Magnet', 'Dove', 'Express', 'Gipsy King' and many others.

Pony traps were also available for private or station work.

Besides the buses to Truro, every Friday there was a trip to St Austell Market. It was always well loaded with large baskets of butter, eggs and poultry,

Fore Street, Tregony circa 1906. AF 189, a Hallamshire, 24 h.p. car registered to Mr Tom Blamey of Veryan drives down through the Village.

and mostly farmers' wives, some of whom sat in the Market House, which was really a Market House in those days, with nearly all farm produce and of course the butchers. I never understood why so much of this went to St Austell, but I should fancy the reason was that it was more of an industrial district and the prices and demand were better. The bus left Tregony at 1 p.m. and arrived home again at 10 p.m. It was a slow journey both ways, for a dozen to fifteen passengers carrying large baskets of produce, some more than one, which all had to be stacked on top of the bus. On the return journey they were all full of groceries etc and it was no joke on a wet and windy night, having to get on top with a bull's eye lamp to get the baskets down. The passengers rode all the way, the horses crawling out of St Austell to Rocky Park and on to Carliza Hill, Sticker Hill, Trawnpool Hill and Nettles Quarry Hill. As some passengers had alighted by this time, the load was lighter and from Faircross to Tregony it would be done at a trot. Before I was 13, I drove the two-horse bus to St Austell, as the other two

Outside Cuby House, Tregony approx 1915, AF 1355, a Slav motor car, first registered in 1914 to Giles Thomson of Cuby House. The gent sitting in the car is Edgar Lidgey who used to drive for the owner.

Fore Street, Tregony – early 1900s. A waggon belonging to A.D. Brewer & Sons of Grampound Road is delivering goods. Argall postcard

drivers were sick. It was whilst driving to St Austell that I saw my first motor car. It was in the distance near Trelowth and I wondered whether the horses would shy, but they took no notice. The car was an open type containing two men, well wrapped up and wearing caps and gloves, and it seemed to me that the vehicle's speed was not much faster than a trotting horse.

Looking at the list of Carters, one wonders how they made a living. In the first place they usually had an acre or two of land and kept a cow or two and pigs, but mostly by carting stones from the quarries at Carne or Probus to the roadside deposits to be broken with hand hammers; after being broken they were then carried to where required. A load of stones weighed one ton to 25 cwt. There were usually two trips to the quarry per cart per day. There was also the upkeep of the roads such as clearing the piles of weeds etc behind the roadmen, so what took six carts then, one lorry can do today.

Caleb's brother-in-law, Absalom Beard, was a coal merchant who had the use of Caleb's cart and horses; so often I went to Ruan Lanihorne for 10 cwt of coal, all in half hundredweights, since not many people could afford the 1/3d per cwt. At that time barges used to come to Ruan Lanihorne with coal, manure, etc and farmers sent their corn away by those barges. Also, at Ruan, was a man called Solly Blamey who had a little steamboat ferry on which he took any passengers to Truro, according to the tides.

Another kind of transport we must not forget is the donkey. Incredibly as it seems today, they did perform a useful service to small traders, postmen and

Ruan Lanihorne in the early 1900s. Mr Solly Blamey and his ferryboat, 'The Amy' taking passengers to Truro.

workers generally. Some would fetch their coal from Ruan Lanihorne, a load being 2½ cwt. When I went with another boy it took us about three hours for the journey. A donkey and trap would also be hired for pleasure to go to the beach for 1/6d per day, 'drive yourself'. My mother and her neighbour and children went once or twice, putting the kettles, sticks and food in the trap whilst we all had alternate rides, what we called 'ride and tie'. I am sure we were more hours on the road than on the beach, but we did enjoy it. I think we enjoyed it as much as the children today on the buses, because we did not go more than once a year anyway.

The choirs of the Churches went to Falmouth, Fowey or Newquay for their outings, but not the Sunday Schools. They had a Tea Treat at home with a brass band to lead the parade through the streets, thence to a field for sports.

I suppose bicycles may be called transport, but the first that I can remember were 'boneshakers'. There were only two – handmade by W. Barnicoat, a carpenter. They had wood spokes in the wheels and

Tregony approx 1910. The man is believed to be Mr Solomon Mountstephens (sen).

45

Tregony circa 1900. Mr John Grose (old gent with beard) is in charge of his son's (Charles Grose) donkey cart. The man standing behind old John bears a resemblance to Bertie Gerrans.

Outside the King's Arms, Tregony 1915~16. A group, possibly the 'Band of Hope' is getting ready to move off. Persons identified are l-r, (drivers on the carts) Moses Barnicoat, Sim Stephens, Charlie Ford? Members of the Spear and Keast families are also present.

light iron bends (or tyres as they call them today). These were followed by the 'penny-farthings' with one large and one small wheel, now museum pieces only. I have seen them being ridden but often wondered how a man could ride them after having an extra pint or two. I'll bet it was an amusing sight, but more about that later. There were also the old three-wheel tricycles, quite comfortable I think, though slow but sure. These models were eventually followed by the type now used, but of course were much heavier with plunger brakes and cushioned tyres.

It was about 1897 when I saw the first pneumatic and free-wheel bikes and at that time, ladies started to ride. The older women didn't like it much. They said it did not look

This 1910 photo shows William Frederick Chenoweth outside his home at Ruan Highlanes near Tregony. Sadly, he features again later in this chapter under tragic circumstances

nice, because those were the days of long skirts and high button boots, but of course the bikes were fitted with a net over the back wheel to prevent their skirts from getting entangled. The older women had another fright a little later when they saw a man and a woman on one bike riding down Tregony Hill. I can fancy them saying, "Gaw, whatever is the world coming to." However, it was only a tandem and I believe it was about that time that ladies took to wearing divided skirts or bloomers, as they were called. (Gaw, I wonder what those dear old ladies would say today, don't you?)

Other Facts & Figures on Transport

Local Information on Lidgey's Coaches. Kelly's Trade Directory of 1910 gave the names of two separate omnibus companies working at Tregony. One was owned by Mr C. Greet and the other by Mr C. Lidgey. In 1915, Caleb Greet was killed whilst on active service in the First

Boscawen Street, Truro 1920s. In the background can be seen one of Lidgey's early motor omnibuses. Unknown source

World War and his business was purchased by the other proprietor, Mr Charles Lidgey. Included in the acquisition was a parcel of land and a shed which were located just below The Square, and on the opposite side of the road to Eadies Court. Thus began the era of the well-known Tregony Bus Company, 'Lidgey's Coaches'. This land was the base for the Lidgey head-quarters and garage. In addition to his buses, Mr Lidgey also owned a smaller waggonette and a horse-drawn hearse. In 1921, horsepower gave way to the petrol engine and soon the first motor omnibuses were travelling the old routes. The Company prospered and continued until 1984 when the present family members retired and the business was sold. The buses with Lidgey's name upon them were in use until the early 1990s. The vacant garage premises were sold in about 1999 and the site developed for housing.

[Interestingly, in December 1920, Mr Lidgey (Senior) was involved in a serious road accident whilst driving his horse bus at Dabb's Hill and it was soon after this that Lidgey's first motor coach was purchased. These two events were suitably recorded in separate issues of 'Tregoney Happenings'].

Royal Cornwall Gazette – 5th Jan 1921
'The friends of C. Lidgey will all be very sorry,
That he got run into by a big lorry,
His conveyance was smashed and the horses knocked down,
And he had to abandon his journey to town'.

Royal Cornwall Gazette – 4th May 1921
'Charlie's 'Sharry-Bang' is bang up to date,
And we make our journeys now in state;
One remarked to me, "I'll tell-ee Boss,
Tes better than riding behind a hoss".

Newspaper Items of the Time

Royal Cornwall Gazette – 2nd July 1896
Teaching Lady to Ride a Bike

'Take the pupil out on a quiet road or lane, one having a gentle incline, preferably, at first. After assisting her to mount from the left side, let her have full control of the steering from the very first, the teacher balancing the machine from the back of the saddle or by a band (not hand!) round the rider's waist, but on no account should the machine and rider be held up forcibly by the handles and saddle, or the operation of teaching will be a lengthy one. Impress on the learner's mind that when she feels the machine has an inclination to fall to the left, she should turn the steering wheel slightly in the same direction, and not in the opposite direction as a learner at first generally does. As the pupil progresses, gradually lessen the

Circa 1917, outside Tregenna Villa (42, Fore Street), Tregony. Mr Preston Tonkin and his wife Selma (nee Harris) on their Sarolea motorcycle & sidecar, visiting her parents.

support given to the machine until it is running unsupported without her knowing it, but run behind the machine to be in readiness to give support if necessary. The machine, at the first few attempts, should be adjusted with the saddle rather low – this will give confidence to the rider – but when able to mount, dismount and ride unaided, the saddle should be raised to its proper height. To mount, have the machine so that the right pedal is just about to descend, hold the handle, place the right foot on the right pedal, put your weight on it, and raise yourself into the saddle. To dismount, wait till the left pedal is just about to descend, put your weight on it, and bring the right foot over the left side'.

Royal Cornwall Gazette – 13th Sept 1900
Cycling Fatality at Tregoney (summary)

'On Monday afternoon, Mr E.L. Carlyon, County Coroner, held an Inquest at the Gregor Arms, Tregoney, touching the death of Joseph Jolly, aged 19 years, a French Cook at the Headland Hotel, Newquay. On Sunday morning, the deceased together with a colleague, Autard Marius, had been cycling down Dabbs Hill, leading to the Town when the left pedal of Jolly's machine came off. Riding a racer without brakes (probably a fixed wheel) he lost control of the mount, which dashed at a terrific rate down the hill. Near the bottom, the hill terminates in an ugly dip with two sharp turns, one of which the deceased negotiated, but at the next he crashed into the hedge and was found by his companion lying in the road terribly maimed and unconscious. He was removed to the Gregor Arms and died in a few minutes. The Coroner said the deceased did not know the road and was riding a machine totally unfitted for the dreadful hills in that part of the County. The Jury returned a verdict of 'accidental death'.

Royal Cornwall Gazette – 9th Feb 1905
Sad Fatality at Tregony

'William Arthur Dowrick, the four-year-old son of George Dowrick, Tregoney, met with a terrible death on Monday morning. A traction engine with two trucks, belonging to Messrs Thomson Bros., was travelling through the Village at a rate of two miles an hour just as the children were leaving the school. Deceased passed between the trucks and tried to get hold of the couplings but was struck on the head and knocked down. The wheels passed along his body and but for the promptitude of the driver in stopping the engine, it would have passed over his head. The engine had to be reversed before the body could be removed and life was then quite extinct. A bystander named Peter Teague picked up the body, which had been mutilated almost beyond recognition and had covered the place with blood. He placed the lifeless burden on the footpath and there it remained for some minutes before the crowd could identify it. Mr E.L. Carlyon held an Inquest on Tuesday. Stephen Dowrick, who witnessed the accident, said there was not the slightest blame attached to the driver (Edward Grose), who was one of the most careful drivers in the district. The jury returned a verdict of 'accident death' and exonerated the driver from blame'.

[As a matter of interest, the West Briton Newspaper, which also reported the same accident, gave the name of the driver as John Pethick].

Royal Cornwall Gazette – 20th Sept 1906
Sad Accident at Tregoney

'A youth named Spear, cycling down Fore Street, on Monday night, collided with a young woman named Polly Adams, aged 20, a niece of Mr Albert J. Harris, draper, and a native of Longton, Staffs. She was thrown violently to the ground sustaining a fractured skull and lies in a precarious condition'.

Royal Cornwall Gazette – 26th Sept 1912
Tregoney

'Mrs Vincent, wife of Mr Thomas Vincent of Barrick, met with a severe accident of Friday. She was journeying to St Austell in Mr Greet's bus when Miss Thomson of Tregonhayne, offered her a seat in her trap and in alighting from the bus she fell forward on to the shafts of the trap and broke her arm, close to the elbow. She was taken on to St Austell and was attended to by Dr Oliver'.

Royal Cornwall Gazette – 5th Dec 1912
Sad Fatality at Tregoney (Summary)

'A collision between a motor car and a motor cycle at the top of Freewater Hill near Tregoney on Tuesday morning, whereby William Frederick Chenoweth, 29 yrs, a motor mechanic carrying on business in Truro with Mr P.T. Hore, and residing at Ruanlanihorne, sustained terrible injuries from which he died, was inquired into at the Royal Cornwall Infirmary yesterday by Mr E.L. Carlyon (Coroner) and a jury. Mr F. Parkin represented Lady Molesworth, whose car was in the collision. The Coroner said the deceased was in the habit of coming from his home into Truro on a motor cycle and on Tuesday he had passed up the hill which leads passed Cornelly Church and across the cross

Another photo of Mr William F Chenoweth. In 1912 he died as a result of a motor accident at Freewater Hill whilst riding a motorcycle.

roads before he got to Freewater Hill. Directly he got on the decline he saw the car driven by Lady Molesworth's chauffeur and slightly altered his course, but coming at such a pace he was unable to alter it enough and instead of running to the rear of the car he struck it amidships. Cycle and car were very badly injured [damaged] and Chenoweth died in the Infirmary without regaining consciousness. After hearing evidence from witnesses, the jury returned a verdict of 'accidental death' and exonerated the chauffeur from all blame'.

Royal Cornwall Gazette – 20th Feb 1913

'Police Sergeant Kendall of Tregoney was on Thursday cycling from Ladock to Grampound Road, when his machine broke in two and he was thrown heavily to the ground. Dr Bonar was summoned and found Mr Kendall partly unconscious and suffering from some severe bruises. He was removed home in a cab and is still suffering from shock'.

Royal Cornwall gazette – 28th Sept 1921
Alarming Accident near Tregoney

'A very alarming accident occurred at Dabb's Hill, last Wednesday afternoon, when a County Council traction engine drawing two trucks of stone from a Probus quarry to Bessy Beneath, Veryan, turned over as result of a skid whilst descending the grade. George Bargett from Tresillian (the driver) and Henry Hawken of Probus (steersman) stuck to their posts and did their best to control the engine. They had a miraculous escape when it toppled over. Both men and T. Shears, who was riding on a truck, escaped with a severe shaking. The road was completely blocked until 1 a.m. on Thursday and Police Sgt Ashford made arrangements for the diversion of traffic. This hill is notorious as one of the most dangerous in the County and it is hoped that the new road through Trewarthenick will soon be opened'.

Chapter 4

CHURCH & CHAPELS

The places of worship were four – the Parish Church, Wesleyan, Congregational and Bible Christian Chapels – and each ran a Sunday School.

The Church services were just as they are today. Both the Wesleyans (now Methodist) and the Congregational churches had morning and evening services with Sunday School in the afternoon. The Bible Christians held afternoon and evening services with the Sunday School in the morning. Each Sunday School had a good number of scholars. The Wesleyans and Bible Christians were supplied by a visiting local preacher and with a Circuit Minister; the Congregationalists had a resident Minister. Their Chapel having been founded in 1750 with a seating capacity of 300. The Minister was Mr Eastburn. All the Chapels at this time formed a United Band of Hope, which was a temperance body, and had quite a good following, which was common throughout the country.

St Cuby's Church Steps & Gate circa 1918. In 1965 a road-widening scheme made alterations to the entrance and the steps were set back from the road by 16 ft.

ST CUBY'S, the PARISH CHURCH OF TREGONY
(Tregony St James with Cuby)

I can remember the old Parish Church before it was restored in 1898/1899 by builders from Redruth or Camborne. One of my first responsible

St Cuby's Church, Tregony in the early-1890s. This old photo shows how the Church looked prior to major renovation work in 1898/9. Look carefully and you can see two men to the left of the porch.

St Cuby's in the early 1900s, after the renovations had been completed.

jobs was to drive two horses in a cart (following Caleb in the first), to Grampound Road Railway Station to fetch roofing slates for the new church roof. The old building had no central pillars then, as it had a high, single-gabled roof. Seating was on the old box seats having doors with button fastenings. There was a gallery at the back. In the corner, where the organ now stands, was a private pew, enclosed of course and fitted with nice cushions etc. I suppose that the Mayor and Burgesses sat there at one time, but I only remember the pew as 'Dr. Bennett's'. As a small Sunday School scholar, I sat there for lessons. Another class was in the vestry and another in the choir seats, which were the first two or three in the centre. The organist was Mr R. Real.

The Church was lit by paraffin lamps and heated by a large bogey [heating stove]. This was before the Hart House Fire, of course, because at that time the Church Hall, as it is now known, was the college schoolroom and was in use as such.

Additional Information

It is probable that the present Church stands on the site of Saint Cuby's original settlement. A building for Christian worship has been here since the sixth century. The earliest indication of a stone building is thought to be in the lower part of the north-west wall which is considered to be Norman.[1] Another ancient feature is that of the celebrated, sixth century, 'Cuby Stone' which is embedded into the exterior south-west wall. This is believed to bear the names

Tregony Parish Church group in about 1906. The only persons identified are: the Rev John Fry Reeves (Rector), Mrs Lavinia Perdoe (front, far left), and Miss Alice Greet, (front, far right).

The interior of St Cuby's Church, Tregony, circa 1907. Taken before the organ had been installed.

Early-1890s. This postcard shows how Tregony Church looked from the east, prior to the 1898/9 reconstruction. Argall

Tregony Church in the early 1900s after the renovations had been completed. Note the new double gabled roof.

of the three children of a Romanised Briton, named Ercilincus.

The church is actually situated within the Parish of Cuby which is the rural area of Tregony. Until about 1553, the Parish of Tregony, which included the old Borough, had its own Parish Church, dedicated to St James. This building was situated close to the River Fal at the bottom of the 'Town', yet it was abandoned because of flooding and silting. Thus Cuby Church became the mother church of the united parishes.

The details of the 1828 and the 1898/99 Cuby Church renovations are worth mentioning. Prior to 1828, the building would have looked much the same as it does today, i.e. with a low, double-gabled roof. However, in the late 1820s, the size of the building had to be enlarged to cater for an increase in the 'free sittings' of the congregation from 30 to 290. The walls were made thinner, the roof was raised into a single-gabled structure and a gallery was constructed across the west-end. By the 1890s, serious flaws in the design and structure began to appear.

A Royal Cornwall Gazette article dated 13th May 1897 stated, 'After a time the outer walls began to yield under the pressure of the large roof and later on the roof itself gave trouble. Matters slowly went from bad to worse and a climax was reached in October last when part of the roof fell in. Since then the services have been held in the Parish Rooms. Over the porch an old-fashioned sundial bears the words 'Mind ye Time', but 'Mind ye Head' would be much more appropriate to the situation'.

The cost of the 1898/99 renovation was estimated at £1200 and it restored the building back to its original type of structure by removing the gallery, lowering the roof and resorting to a double-gabled roof. These plans were prepared by Mr J. Piers St Aubyn.

Tregony Methodist Chapel – 1991. Little has altered externally since its construction in 1824. Services are still regularly held in the chapel. The Author

TREGONY WESLEYAN METHODIST CHAPEL & SUNDAY SCHOOL
(Methodist Church)

Additional Information

According to the late Rev Tom Shaw (Methodist Historian), it is probable that the present Methodist Chapel is the third building to have been erected on the site.[2] The 1787 Tregony

Borough Map [3] shows a Methodist Meeting House on the present site which is believed to have been in use for the previous eight years at least. In 1790 a second place of worship was constructed, a fact supported by the Bishop's Licence of 1799, which speaks of 'a lately erected house at Tregony'. Assuming that date is correct, the present Chapel, which opened in 1824, is the third in succession.

A 1960s snapshot of the interior of Tregony Methodist Chapel. The late Mrs Ruby Grigg

Wesleyan Methodist Sunday School Building

The separate Sunday School building was erected in 1883 and was located ten yards further up Fore Street. During the zenith of the Methodist movement, as well as housing the large Sunday School, the building was also regularly used for Chapel events. By the 1990s the Sunday School had finished and the need for the building had ceased. In 1994 it was sold and became a private dwelling.

At the rear of the building, below ground level was a partly covered yard and stable

The old Wesleyan Methodist Sunday School building at Tregony. It was sold in 1994 and is now a private dwelling. The Author 1991

where the horses and traps of some the congregation were left during the services. There was also an old 'dry' lavatory which deposited sand instead of water when the chain was pulled.

West Briton Newspaper (summary)

'On the 27th October 1883 a large number of spectators attended the stone-laying ceremony at the start of the building of the Wesleyan Sunday School. Stones were laid by: Mr W.H.P. Martin, Mayor of Truro; Mr W.H. Trounce of Trevilveth, Veryan, and Mr William Huddy of Nancevallen, Kea. A sum of £6.2s.0d was placed upon the centre stone by Mr F. Chenoweth on behalf of the teachers and scholars, a portion of which was for prizes the children very willingly gave up towards the building fund. Other offerings followed and a collection was made. Adjourned afterwards to the Board School for a tea'.

Tregony Chapel Records – January 1893

'A well-attended meeting of the Trustees of the Wesleyan schoolroom was held on Monday Dec 5th when it was unanimously resolved that the use of the room be granted to the newly formed United Methodist Temperance Society for committee meetings and occasional public meetings'.

Cornwall Methodist Circuit Recorder – April 1894

'Tregony. The harvest festival services were held here on Oct 7th and 8th. Two very enjoyable and profitable services were held on Sunday, and Monday a public tea and after-meeting which were very successful, but unfortunately at Tregony the usual harvest festival decorations had been omitted, and by some these were missed very much, as they left a blank appearance, which good speeches from Chairman Coon and others speakers could not satisfactorily fill'.

Royal Cornwall Gazette – 16th May 1907

Tregony Wesleyans – Opening a New Organ

'On Thursday the Wesleyans of Tregoney had a big day. It opened by a luncheon in the Schoolroom, at which there was a very large attendance, presided over by Mr M. Holman, of Mylor. Later in the day there was a sale of work at the Congregational School, kindly lent for the occasion. During the afternoon recitations and music were given by Mr and Mrs Riley of St Austell and others. After a very largely patronised public tea, a sacred concert was given in the Wesleyan Chapel. Miss Beale played several selections on the new American organ, purchased at a cost of between £50 and £60'.

CONGREGATIONAL CHAPEL
[Sometimes known as the Independent Church]

The Headmaster of Hart House School, the Rev. J. Thompson and his family were the chief supporters of the Congregational Church where they and the scholars attended each Sunday. Some used to call it 'Thompson's Chapel'.

Additional Information

The present Congregational Chapel was erected in 1824, the same date, incidentally, as the Wesleyan Methodist. Previously, the congregation had worshipped in a former building called the 'Presbyterian Meeting House' or sometimes the 'Little Chapel'.[4] This building stood in Tregony Hill, just below The Square on a plot of land on the oppo-

The pulpit of Tregony Congregational Chapel, circa 1915. The banner on the wall reads 'The Lord is in his Holy Temple.'

The Congregational Chapel, Fore Street, Tregony. Built in 1824 the Chapel is still used regularly for worship. The Author 1991

Mr Arthur Ince, his wife and son, Gordon. He was the Pastor in Charge of the Tregony and Grampound Congregational Chapels from 1912 to 1917.

site side of the road to Eadies Court.

In 1822, Dr James Hart from St Austell took over the Ministry of the Chapel. Also he opened a small private boarding school at his home in the middle of the town. (Later the School moved to premises at the top of the town and became known as Hart House School). This was the start of a close affinity between the Chapel and School which was to last for 60 years. In 1861 the Rev. John Thompson took over both School and Chapel. The School was a major influence on the community and Chapel. Pupils regularly swelled the numbers of the congregation with 'youthful vigour and angelic voices'.

It was mainly owing to the Rev Thompson's initiative and generosity that alterations were made and the Sunday School was built in 1882.

On the 7th January 1878, the first wedding was solemnised in the Chapel between Mr Henry Hotten and Miss Amelia Brewer. Three days later the marriage of Mr H.C. Roberts to Miss S.M. Berryman took place.

During 1893, two events of major magnitude in the history of the Church occurred, one glorious, the other catastrophic. On 17th & 18th April the Spring Meetings of the County Union were held in Tregony. They were a huge success, declared to be among the best on record. Ministers and delegates were accommodated in the dormitories at Hart House and received the generous hospitality of the Thompson Family. Mr Eastman the local Minister was elected Chairman of the Union, and Mr Herbert Thompson, Treasurer. Naturally Tregony people were much elated; but only 12 days later, on a Sunday morning, disaster struck; Hart House School was burnt to the ground, leaving a heap of ruins. Within four months of the disaster the Thompsons had left Tregony and their school had vanished. The effects were severely felt in the Village, yet the Chapel survived and slowly scars healed and life resumed.

NEW BIBLE CHRISTIAN CHAPEL
[also known as the Bryanite's Chapel]

A new Bible Christian Chapel was built in the late 1890s, the builders then being Messrs W. GERRANS and Son of Tregony (carpenters) and Messrs DAVEY and Sons of Pentewan (masons). The building being constructed of brick.

Additional Information

The Chapel was situated halfway down Tregony Hill on the right-hand side, just below the old thatched cottage known as Beggers Roost.

Royal Cornwall Gazette – 3rd March 1898

'At the recent laying of the Memorial Stones of the new Bible Christian Chapel at

An early 1900s photo of what is believed to have been the interior of the new Tregony Bible Christian Chapel.

Tregoney, the Rev E.V. Stephens gave a short account of the history in Tregoney. Originally it belonged to the Truro Circuit, but was subsequently erased from the Truro plan. For a time the doors were kept open by three old ladies. Afterwards the chapel was taken over by Mevagissey Circuit. Since that time there has been slow but gradual improvement. The number of sittings let had nearly doubled in three years and a Sunday School, formed three years ago, had now 70 scholars'.

Tregony Bible Christian Chapel in the early 1900s shortly after it had been built on a site in Tregony Hill.

According to the Chapel Account Book[5] – 'This chapel was built in 1898 on a piece of land purchased of Mr Andrew of Ponsanooth. Four memorial stones were laid on Tuesday Feb 15th 1898 by William Martin Esq. (ex Mayor of Bodmin), Mrs M.L. Blamey of Camels (Veryan), Miss H. Blamey of Portloe and Mr J.H. Michell of Cornelly; and a considerable number of bricks were also laid by the village children and interested friends. A tea and public meeting followed. The proceeds of the day amounted to £45, making the total receipts towards the building fund about £85. The chapel is to be built of red and white brick and the estimated cost is about £300'.

Royal Cornwall Gazette - 14th July 1898

'Tregoney Bible Christians having decided to build a new chapel and use the old building for a schoolroom. The 5th inst. witnessed the practical completion of the scheme. The new building is 34 feet by 24 feet. The cost, including a freehold site, is over £300. The architect is the Rev E.V. Stephens, the Pastor. The President of the Conference, Rev A. Trengrove, conducted a dedication service in the morning. After the service there was a public luncheon in the Congregational School-room followed by another service at 3 p.m. in the new chapel, together with a public tea and a further meeting'.

The Trustees were ever watchful over the costs. At a meeting in March 1899 it was recorded, 'Mr. Stephens was appointed to see Mr Gerrans [carpenter] about his bill, the

A 1991 photo of the Bible Christian building as it looks today. The gentleman standing in the adjoining garden is the late Mr Henry Biddick. The Author

Trustees considered there was too much charged for extras. Also Mr Michell's [blacksmith] bill for railings and gate; the Trustees considered it an over-charge'.

At the July 1899 meeting the following was endorsed, 'Mr Stephens having seen Mr Gerrans respecting his bill, awarded for extras, £3.10s instead of £7.1s.0d. and Michell £10.10s'.

September 1907 marked the date when the Bible Christian Connexion joined with the Methodist New Connexion and the United Methodist Free Churches to form the 'United Methodist Church'.

In the mid-1920s, my Mother, Mrs Ruby Grace Grigg (neé Barnicoat), then a young girl, attended this Chapel with her family. Her mother, Mrs Ethel Barnicoat, a music teacher, used to play the harmonium organ at the services. The Chapel did not stay in existence for many more years and it closed in approximately 1930, when my mother was about ten years old.

The Chapel is believed to have been short-lived owning to lack of support. However, 1932 brought another Methodist merger which incorporated many splintered factions, including the United Methodists (previous Bible Christians), under the umbrella of the new, 'Methodist Church'. Many of the smaller chapels were closed. My family moved to the larger, Tregony (ex-Wesleyan) Methodist Chapel.

The property deeds[6] confirmed that Mr & Mrs Edward (Tommy) Grose bought the vacant (B.C.) chapel on the 8th November 1933. The building was converted into a dwelling and it still serves the same purpose today.

THE ORIGINAL BIBLE CHRISTIAN CHAPEL

Additional Information

The 1898 chapel was not the first Bible Christian building in Tregony. Sixty yards further down Tregony Hill and on the same side, can still be seen today, the shell of the original Meeting House which is believed to have been built in the early 1830s. It is attached to a dwelling named Ivy Cottage, which at one time was considered to be the home of the chapel caretaker. Access via an external passageway between the two buildings led to the rear of the old chapel and its store and toilet.

Most certainly, meetings were held prior to 1830, but they were probably conducted in private houses. In an 1828 letter addressed to Loveday Sarah Gregor, the Mistress of Trewarthenick of Cornelly, it was stated, 'John Hunkin and his wife are very partial to attend the Bryanites meetings at Tregony'.[7] Later in the same letter it described the chapel members as being, 'more like maniacs than reasonable beings', because of their enthusiastic manner of worship.

The remains of the original Tregony Bible Christian Meeting House, situated in Tregony Hill, below the later Chapel. The Author 1992

According to the Religious Census of 1851,[8] the Rev William Wellington, the Bible Christian Minister from Truro, stated that the Tregony Chapel was erected in 1834. Further confirmation of the proximity of this date, was provided in the 1836 Will of Robert Luke of Tregony.[9] He bequeathed 'the lands on which the Meeting House is built to the Society of Bible Christians to be held by them in fee forever', etc. The Bible Christians, who were known for their devout temperance and simplicity, worshipped in a vigorous and impassioned manner.

Sundays in those days were very quiet indeed. All shutters would be put up on the shop windows on Saturday nights and no dealings would be done on Sundays, except in the case of emergency. Most people, whether they went to a place of worship or not, would not do much on a Sunday. In fact, the majority did go at least once a Sunday to a Service; otherwise there would not have been such beautiful chapels, and I doubt if there is any old village of the size of Tregony that had better buildings or congregations.

There was very little traffic on Sundays; no carts or waggons, only a few farmers coming to Church or Chapel in their traps or carriages or maybe the Doctor, or someone going courting at St Austell (or further afield) or folk visiting sick relatives. Apart from these, there were just the villagers moving around to Church or Chapel or maybe the pubs – they had their regulars then, as now.

There were no Sunday papers at this time, but there were religious tracts given out by ladies on Sunday afternoons. These books were exchangeable each week. It was not until about 1900 that the first Sunday papers were introduced.

On Sundays it was the custom to take walks around the various lanes and also to view the various crops and gardens because a far greater interest was taken in gardens and allotments in those days, as practically everyone grew most of the produce they required. One thing that struck me about Sundays, was the gathering of all the youths and maidens after evening services. They had a sort of parade along the Woods End Road, at Cornelly, where they had their bit of fun, laughing and joking, but the young men and boys would join together and sing hymns, mostly of the Revival type.

References

1   Cuby Parish Church Guidebook 1960 - copy with the Author.

2   The Shaw Methodist Collection – Courtney Library, Royal Institution of Cornwall.

3   1787 Tregony Borough Map – Cornwall Record Office DDJ1516.

4   Notes of the Centenary Address at Tregony Congregational Chapel 1924 – copy with the Author.

5   Copy of the Tregony Bible Christian Chapel Account Book 1898 to 1930 – copy with the Author.

6   Deeds of the B.C. Chapel Building in possession of Mr Alan Grose

7   'Veryan & the Roseland' - booklet by Christine Hawkridge 1967.

8   Non-Conformist Census for Tregony 1851 – Cornwall Record Office FS/2/94/1.

9   Will of Robert Luke of Tregony 1836 – Cornwall Record Office AP/L/2364.

Chapter 5

1840s–1893

Additional Information

A stranger visiting Tregony today would find little evidence to support the fact that a large, well-known, 19th century, boys' boarding school ever existed there. The only clue is a 1930s bungalow (recently renovated), with a terraced, front garden, which is situated at the top of the village immediately below the Parish Church. The bungalow, aptly named 'Hart-Lea' was erected on the former site of 'Hart House School'.

Hart House School, Tregony. An early 1890s photo looking up Fore Street towards the Church.

'Hart Lea' Bungalow is visible on the site of Hart House School, peeping out from behind the white cottage. The Author 1997

In 1818, a large house had recently been constructed there as a private dwelling for the Reverend Richard Gurney, the then Rector and Chief Magistrate of the Borough of Tregony. This building was named Trewinion House.[1]

In 1822, Dr James HART [2], a dissenting minister of the Independent (Congregational) Church, moved to Tregony from St Austell to take up his post at the Town Chapel. He also opened a small private school for young gentlemen at his house in the centre of the Village. In the early 1840s he took over the possession of Trewinion House and opened a larger, independent, fee-paying, boys' academy for boarders and daily attendees. It officially became known as Hart House School although the locals called it 'the Mansion'. After James Hart died in 1844 his son, the Rev. Baron Hart ran the school. In 1861, the Rev. John Thompson took over the ownership. All the proprietors were ministers of the local Congregational Chapel. The School and its students were an integral part of the Chapel and local community.

The School, which catered for the social needs of young, middle-class, gentlemen, aged between 8 and 18 years, provided a curriculum designed to fulfil the educational requirements of the period. An 1878 advertisement taken from Harrod's Directory [3] of Cornwall describes the school as the "largest middle-class boarding school in Cornwall affording an excellent education to about 100 pupils."

By 1871, the school building had been extended and extra domestic and teaching staff

Hart House School circa 1890, seen from the St Austell direction.

A 1960s snapshot of Hart Lea, looking from the direction of St Austell. The late Mark Jacob

employed to cope with the increased numbers of scholars which had risen to approximately 100 mixed boarders and local day pupils.

The school continued to prosper until the early morning of Sunday, 30th April 1893, when a catastrophe overtook it. The school building caught fire and it was completely destroyed. Fortunately, there were no casualties. A full and very descriptive article about the fire was reported in the West Briton Newspaper.

Article in the West Briton Newspaper – 4th May 1893 (2nd edition)

DISASTROUS FIRE IN TREGONY – HART HOUSE DESTROYED
Estimated Damage over £4000

REV. J. THOMPSON.

Hart House School,
TREGONEY, CORNWALL
CONDUCTED BY THE

REV. J. THOMPSON,
Assisted by a Competent Staff of Masters.

SYNOPSIS—

Intellectual Instruction—Reading and Elocution ; Writing—Plain, Ornamental, and Commercial ; Grammar and Composition ; Geography, with Mapping ; Ancient and Modern History ; Arithmetic and Mental Calculations ; Algebra ; Euclid's Geometry ; Trigonometry ; Mensuration—with Land Surveying taught practically ; Lectures on various branches of Science.

Moral Training—Religious Instruction ; Moral and Scripture Lessons ; daily attention to the cultivation of the Moral Sentiments, Good Habits, and Correct Manners and Deportment.

Physical Training and Health—Drill ; Playground and Cricket Field ; Diet—substantial, varied, and unlimited. The Domestic Arrangements are under Mrs. Thompson's personal superintendence, and are such as to secure the comfort of the Pupils.

TERMS—

YEARLY BOARDERS ...	... ...	... 30 GUINEAS PER ANNUM.
DITTO DITTO UNDER TEN YEARS	... 25	,, ,, ,,

These terms include General Instruction, Board, Laundress, use of Books, supply of School Stationery, Drill, and Pew Rent.

The only Extra Charges are the following—

LATIN, GREEK, FRENCH, GERMAN, AND DRAWING, EACH	... 2 GUINEAS PER ANNUM.
MUSIC, WITH USE OF PIANO	... 5 ,, ,, ,,

An advertisement from the 1878 edition of Harrod's Cornwall Trade Directory.

'Few houses are better known by repute than Hart House, Tregony, which has for at least 80 years been the home of an important Boarding School, formerly conducted by the Rev Thomas Baron Hart (and previously by his father), and for the past 32 years by the Rev J. Thompson. Hart House is now, we much regret to state, nothing but a pile of ruins, the premises having been completely gutted by fire which occurred yesterday morning [*Sunday, 30th April 1893*]. The house was originally built for the accommodation of 100 boarders and up to within a week or so ago there were 45 in residence, in addition to the family, the teachers and servants. Fortunately, however, the bulk of the scholars are presently enjoying a vacation at their respective homes. Only 13 in fact were actually in residence and this is a matter for devout thankfulness, for the dormitories were completely destroyed; and if the full number of boys had been on the premises, the consequences might have been far more serious than they are, seeing that the fire broke out at a time when probably the whole of them would have been in bed. From the account which follows, it will be seen that, as it is, the results are of a very serious character and we are quite sure that in the calamity which has befallen them, Mr and Mrs Thompson and their family have the sympathy of the Cornish folk generally.

Hart House, it will be remembered, stood at the very top of Tregony Town, close to the entrance of Cuby Parish Church.

Truro received the news of the fire on Sunday morning between 8 and 9 o'clock, a telegraphic despatch being received at the Railway Station from Grampound Road, summoning the Fire Brigade. The summons was conveyed to Truro Police Station and immediately the electric bells which are connected with the residences of the firemen, were rung. The response to the call was, as usual, prompt and within a few minutes all was excitement at the Fire Station. Mr F. Holman, of Lemon Mews, who now has the horsing of the engines, was soon in attendance with two horses. These were attached to one of the engines, and Lieut. Carlyon in command, a start was made about 25 minutes to nine for the scene of the fire. Seeing that the road to Tregony is a very hilly one, it was thought that two horses were insufficient for the engine, and two others were

The ruins of Hart House School after the disastrous fire in 1893.

fetched from Mr Holman's. These overtook the brigade about a mile and a half from Truro, and being attached to the engine, Tregony was soon reached. A second engine, drawn by four horses, also started at 9 o'clock from Truro, Lieut. Rice being in command. Arriving at Tregony, the Brigade saw that the main building was burnt to the ground, but set to work with all speed with a view to saving a small

The only part of Hart House School which survived the fire was the detached classroom. After the fire this building was used as the Parish Rooms and is now known as the Church Hall. The Author 1996

building adjoining, in which they were successful. Within fifty minutes of the alarm being given, the first engine was at work, and rendering every possible assistance. As is generally the case in small places, there was a scarcity of water and the recent long drought had, of course, made the state of things in this direction worse than usual. One well soon emptied, and recourse was made to another, but soon this one gave out. Then no less than 2000 feet of hose had to be put together to reach a third well. The Brigade, although unable, in consequence of lack of water, to extinguish the fire, rendered valuable assistance in preventing

(41 Fore Street)
The **SICKBAY** was located on the 1st floor.
The **STABLE** & **COACH-HOUSE** were on the ground floor.

(Cuby Cottage)
The **LAUNDRY**.
2 ladies who resided in one of the two original cottages worked as laundresses

(Pine Cottage)
A small **SHOP** used by the scholars as a tuck shop

(Hart Lea Bungalow)
The site of
HART HOUSE SCHOOL

A photo taken from the church tower showing the location of the old school site and other buildings that were associated with the school. The Author 2000

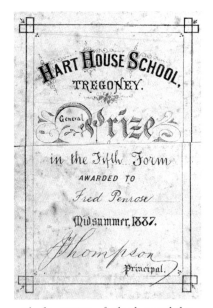

The frontispiece of a book awarded to Fred Penrose in 1887. (The Works of Shakespeare). Frederick Penrose aged about 15 yrs, was a boarder whose home was at Helston. He died in 1914.

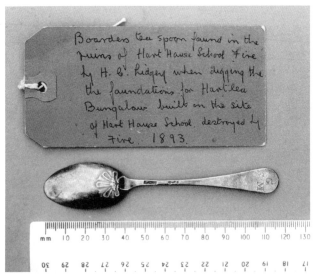

This spoon was recovered from the site of the old school in the 1930s. The initials inscribed on the spoon are 'S.G.M.'. The 1891 Census showed Stanley G Murray, 12 yrs as a boarder at Hart House School. His family came from Gateshead in Durham.
The Author 2000

the flames from spreading. In a very short time, the building was completely gutted and the blackened walls threatened every moment to collapse. To guard against any mishap from these suddenly falling, ropes were thrown through the windows and over the top, and the front portion of the building was pulled down. The work of demolition was watched by a large crowd, composed of villagers and those who had come from Truro and the surrounding neighbourhood. There was great excitement as the walls fell with a crash to the ground, those standing near being for a moment enveloped in dense clouds of dust. There being nothing further for the Brigade to do, a start was made shortly before three for Truro, which was reached three-quarters of an hour later.

From information obtained by our representative, it appears that about 7 o'clock on Sunday morning, Mrs Eliza Grose was proceeding to her work at Tregonhayne, the house of Mr Peter Thompson, a farmer, when, on passing Hart House, she noticed smoke issuing from the roof of the building. Thinking something was wrong, she rang the bell and called the attention of a man named John Beard to the smoke. Slates immediately com-

menced falling from the roof and then it was seen that a fire was raging in the
upper part of the building. An alarm was at once raised, and soon the villagers
rushed from their houses and lent all assistance in their power to save whatever
property they could. Mr James Stephens of the Post Office was at once appraised
of the fire, and he telephoned to Grampound Road from whence the summons
for the Fire Brigade was communicated to Truro. There is no telegraphic or telephone communication between Truro and Tregony, so that Mr Stephens had no
alternative but to communicate by way of Grampound Road. Soon after the dis-
covery of the fire, the building was ablaze from end to end, and efforts could only
be made to save the furniture and other contents. A considerable quantity of
property was saved, although a large portion was destroyed, also some jewellery
and other valuables belonging to Mr and Mrs Thompson, their family and to the
boys. Mr Thompson lost his gold watch and chain; Mrs Thompson's loss included her rings; one of the scholars also lost a watch; and others all their wearing
apparel, with their boxes. The origin of the fire appears to be a mystery, but it
was stated that the kitchen flue was connected with the flue in Mr Thompson's
bedroom; and seeing that it was in the roof over this bedroom where the fire was
first discovered, the idea is that the kitchen flue got over-heated and so caused
the fire.

Mr Thompson himself stated that, as usual, he went round the house the last
thing on Saturday night before retiring to bed and put out all the lights.
Everything seemed safe, and there was not the slightest sign of fire. All went well
until 7 o'clock in the morning when a ring was heard at the door bell and slates
were heard falling from the roof. On looking out he saw his servant man with a
frightened expression on his face looking towards the house. Immediately one of
the servants rushed into the room and said the house was on fire. Mrs
Thompson, who had been the first to wake, at once commenced dressing, and Mr
Thompson, having put on a few things, went to where the boys were sleeping,
but found they had already been appraised of the fire and were hastily making
arrangements to leave the building. Mr Thompson instructed them to get all they
could into their boxes – at the same time assisting them to do so – and leave by
the north door. The boys did this and most of them were successful in saving
their belongings, although two or three of them had their boxes with their contents destroyed. The fire was raging in the upper part of the building and this
allowed the many willing helpers, who had by this time arrived, to save a considerable portion of the furniture and other valuable property. Mr Thompson
estimates the damage at between £4000 and £5000 but fortunately the loss is

largely covered by insurance in the London, Liverpool and Globe Office. Mr Thompson spoke highly of the ready assistance rendered by the villagers, who were instrumental in greatly lessening his losses.

Hart House, as previously stated, has been in possession of Mr Thompson for the last 32 years, the school being conducted by himself and his son, Mr H.J. Thompson, M.A., assisted by other teachers. The re-assembling of the school was to have taken place on Tuesday, but of course this could not be, and Mr Thompson notified the position of the affairs to the parents and asked that the boys may be kept at home another week or so, while arrangements are being made for their accommodation. The schoolroom itself, which is detached from the other buildings, fortunately escaped the fire, so that the desks, books and other schoolroom requisites are all saved'.

The end

The fire which destroyed Hart House School in 1893 and which caused its closure was a tragic event in the Village as a school of 40 boarders meant much to the trade and communal life of the Village. Attending the school were also some 'day boys' from farms and neighbouring villages, some of whom came on ponies. Naturally there was a fairly large staff - eight indoors, one gardener and a handyman and a youth for the horse and the smallholding adjoining, where cows, pigs and poultry were kept to supply the household. The school also provided work for a shoemaker, Mr David Barnicoat, and others; also for the bus proprietor, providing transport for the school such as the cricket, football and rugby teams. In addition, the Thompsons provided free soup daily to any elderly or sick who cared to fetch it, as did the Rector, the Rev J.F. Reeves at the Rectory.

Additional Information

Although the School closed, initially great efforts were undertaken to continue educating the scholars at Tregony. The Royal Cornwall Gazette of the 18th May 1893 reported – 'The temporary buildings which have been erected for the reception of the pupils were opened on Tuesday, for the re-assembling of the school. A large gang of workers have made much progress. The large classroom, which escaped destruction, has been converted into dormitories, which are occupied by the junior principal and all the elder students. All walls in the front of the old house have been lowered to one storey and roofed in to make dining-hall, schoolroom, kitchens, pantries and offices. There will be no difficulty in carrying on the school as usual'.

However, by September of 1893, the Principal had decided not to rebuild the old school, and to relocate to a new site at Burnham in Somerset.

The only beneficial legacy for Tregony from the closure of the school was the recreational use of the old Hart House 'playing field' as the Tregony Sports field. Amongst other facilities, the prepared cricket square, which had been laid during the time of the College, is still being used today.

A final postscript on the subject: in April of 1895, Mr D. Barnicoat, a shoemaker of Tregony, filed for bankruptcy and cited as a reason, "the School being removed to Somersetshire took away nearly the whole of his trade."

Royal Cornwall Gazette – 20th August 1919
A Tregoney Epitaph

Our Tregony correspondent sent the following inscription from a stone in the churchyard:

"Weep not for me you standers by,
As you are now so once was I;
As I am now so must you be,
So prepare for death and follow me."

Some years ago an old Hart House scholar pencilled in the following underneath the inscription:

"To follow you is not my intent,
For I do not know which way you went."

References

1 'The Gurney Family' 1887, an unpublished account - copy with the Author.
2 Notes on the Tregony Congregational Chapel Centenary Address 1924 - copy with the Author.
3 Harrod's Trade Directory 1878 - The Cornwall Centre.

Chapter 6

THE VILLAGE & VILLAGE LIFE

I will try to explain just how it looked in those days. Apart from the new hous-es built since the last war [*Second World War*], known as the 'the Crescent', [*Roseland Crescent*], only three new houses and one bungalow have been built since the *1890s* and they are on sites where former houses existed. In the main, therefore, Tregony Fore Street, from the Church to the Bridge, has not altered. It may be that a few houses have been re-conditioned and many of the old thatched roofs have been slated, about 12 in all in Fore Street. By and large, very little change has taken place in the structural sense, while the condition of the houses and outside appearance have been greatly improved. In fact, there is no compari-son between then and now. The roads and pavements in those days were uneven and muddy at times, with pools of water. The pavements were rough and the kerb stones irregular. Many of the houses had pebbled pavements, no doubt placed there by the owner and these were the better class houses in the by-gone days.

Postcard of the Village Square at Tregony in 1950. George Ellis Collection, The Cornwall Centre.

This lop-sided snapshot shows how the other side of the Village Square looked in the 1930s. The Author

It is not generally known by the younger generation that what is now referred to as 'The Square', in those days was known as 'The Bank' and all meetings or open-air services would be advertised as such, but why it was called 'The Bank', I never knew.

Looking back at the mid-*1890s*, there are some bright spots; one being the new bridge across the 'white river' which was built in 1893 by Cornwall County Council, the builder being a Tregony contractor, a Mr R.H. Tonkin. The old bridge was very narrow indeed, and had lay-bys for pedestrians to allow traffic to pass.

In 1895, because they had become completely dilapidated, the Hugh Boscawen Alms Houses were restored, the contractors being Mr W. Hugh of Veryan (mason) and Mr Blamey of Portloe (carpenter). There are six apartments for elderly ladies: the first six ladies were – Miss Jane Sim, Mrs Peters, Mrs Nancy Burley, Miss Ruth Banfield, Mrs Ann Woolcock and Mrs Corkhill. (I just mentioned these for the local interest).

Additional Information

In point of fact the Almshouses, or the 'Gallery' as it is locally known, was built in 1696 by Hugh Boscawen M.P., to house "10 indigent housekeepers" of Tregony. In 1867 the Boscawen Charity consisted of 90 acres real estate and £400 stock, the gross income of which was

The old Tregony Bridge approx 1892. The horse bus 'named 'The Telephone' is en route to Truro. In the foreground workmen are in the initial stages of the construction of the new bridge.
CRO-(X230/57/3/156)

Tregony Bridge 1893. The new bridge is progressing well. The old bridge is still in use and can be seen in the background with a horse and cart crossing it. CRO-(X230/57/3/158)

Tregony Almshouses, early 1900s; locally named the 'The Gallery'. The adjoining building was the old Tregony Borough Jail. Further down is a row of old, single storied, properties, once known as the 'Poor Houses' which today are private dwellings called 'Castle View'.

applied in support of almshouse, the inmates and pensioners.

Because the structure of the 'Gallery' had been allowed to become so neglected, the 1881 and 1891 Censuses [1] confirmed that the property was uninhabited. Prior to its restoration in 1895, only the walls and the two chimney ends were standing.

The Boscawen Charity Trustee's Minute Book [2] reported that as far back as July 1872, the topic of whether the Almshouse should be entirely rebuilt or simply repaired was discussed. It transpired that only basic repairs were carried out. By August of 1875 the conditions had deteriorated so much that the Rev J.M. Manford, Curate of Tregony, complained that, because of the wet and miserable surroundings, the present number of residents had reduced from ten to five.

On the 6th March 1876, the minutes recorded that, 'It was proposed and carried, that considering the unsecured and dangerous condition of the old Almshouses, it is deemed necessary that, (1) they at once be taken down and new buildings erected in the stead; (2) Mr Trevail, architect, of St Blazey be instructed to prepare plans/specifications and (3) meanwhile, the inmates be permitted to reside with friends or otherwise at the expense of the Charity'.

Eventually after much discussion with the Charity Commissioners, complete renovation

The rear of 'The Gallery' – 1895. Here workmen are posing after the renovation work had been completed. Solly Mountstephens is the bearded gent holding a trowel, (under the right hand chimney).

of the structure was decided and the number of inmates were reduced from ten to six, none of whom was to be in receipt of Parish Pay. By December of 1895, arrangements were being made to re-occupy the Almshouse rooms.

The Gallery, which is still open today, accommodates six local persons, men and women.

Town Oven

[Located at what is now 'Well Cottage', 5, Well Street].

There cannot be many today who can remember the Oven situated in Well Street and run by Mr Absalom Beard, known as 'Apsie'. It was extensively used, being lit every other day, including Sundays, as quite a number of houses had only a grate and cloam oven. The oven would take about 50 to 60 dishes and to heat the

The old Town Oven in Well Street, Tregony. This recent photo shows the lately named, 'Well Cottage' at number 5. The bakehouse was located in the single storied section and access was gained via the door beside the large window. Immediately outside was the site of a covered well. The Author 2003

oven it took two faggots of wood. When burnt, the oven was ready for the dishes, which all had their private markings, but sometimes mistakes were made and not discovered until the contents were half eaten, which caused heated arguments, as you can guess. Sunday was the big day, when at about 12.30 all concerned would be lined up with their trays and cloths, waiting for the oven to open, when out came the pies, puddings, roasts, etc for which they had paid 1d to 2d per dish.

Additional Information

The bakehouse had obviously been in use for many years. An Abstract of Title document, dated October 1829[3], made reference to a house with a Common Oven in Pig Street." [We now call it Well Street].

In the 1861 to 1881 Tregony Censuses, Peter BEARD, a baker and his family were reported as living in Well Street. By the time of the 1891 Census and through until 1901, Peter's son, Absalom BEARD had taken over the ownership of the premises. The occupation of 'baker' was only given to Absalom in 1881, but that is not to imply that the bakehouse had closed by 1901.

At a public auction held at the Town Arms Hotel, Tregony on the 16th Sept 1911, the fol-

Well Street, Tregony circa 1895, (looking up Well Street towards The Square). The covered well can be seen on the right-hand side with the bakehouse just beyond it. The building on the left is the lodging house run by Miss Jane Sim (2nd from the left). The bowler hatted gent is Absalom Beard.

lowing freehold property was offered: 'A cottage containing six rooms with garden, coalhouse, piggery, bakehouse and yard, situated in Well Street, lately in occupation of Absalom John Beard, deceased. It was purchased for £52 by Mr Beard of Devonport'.

Another Bakehouse?

Information was recently received from Mr Dennis Curtis, that in the 1960s, whilst he was undertaking some internal renovation work on the 'top shop' [now known as No. 53, Fore Street, The Children's Play School], he found the remains of a large conical brick oven. It had been built into a wall but was covered with plaster. The oven measured some four feet wide and about four feet long with a three feet high curved roof which was constructed with bricks. The base was about three feet from the ground.

It can only be supposed that the oven had been used in the early 1900s, when the premises had been a grocer's store, and known as Tonkin's Shop.

Lodging House
[Believed to have been located in what is now known as Vivian House, 7 Well Street]

Whilst in Well Street, let us take a look at the Lodging House which was run by my Great Aunt, Miss Jane Sim. She took in wayfarers at 4d per night, not so much for the money, but because she was a devout Bible Christian and a good samaritan. The house which was then thatched was her own and she also had 4/- per week from the Boscawan Charity. She eventually went to the Almshouses to live when they were restored in 1895. There were all sorts of tramps of almost every nationality in those days, but she never turned one away and was not afraid of anyone. Her one rule was "No Smoking Allowed".

Additional Information

Miss Jane Sim, lodging house keeper of Well Street. Circa 1895.

In the 1891 Census, Miss Jane Sim, aged 75, a lodging house keeper was listed at Well Street. She must have had a quiet day as the only other two people in the house were lodgers: John Carr, aged 60 years, a pedlar by trade, who was born in Newcastle-on-Tyne, and Elizabeth Tregenza' aged 51, a pedlar who was born at Redruth.

It is fascinating to go back a further 10 years to 1881,

to see that the landlady then was a local widow, named Mary Mountstephens, aged 63 years. She had an elderly aunt living with her, who possibly helped her. Mary would have needed all the help she could muster because on the day of the census there were eight German musicians lodging there.

Penlee House

[Now Penlee Residential & Nursing Home]

According to the late Mr K.O. Parsons, (1887–1986)[4], a local amateur historian who lived in the house, it was built about 1838 by the Tregony Borough Corporation for use as a Rectory. The local incumbent's rent was £30 per annum. Tregony, prior to this, did not have a permanent home for its Rector. In 1839, because the Borough Corporation was becoming defunct, most of its properties, including Penlee House, were put up for auction. The House was sold, but with the proviso that the resident Rector, the Rev Lugger, should remain there during his incumbency. The Reverend retired in 1847 whereby the large house became a private residence.

Penlee House, Tregony, circa 1915. The Huddy family. The two persons standing are thought to have been Sampson & Amelia Huddy, brother and sister.

In 1861, the Census showed Dr Charles Bennetts, surgeon, and his family residing there.

In the 1880s, Mr and Mrs John Simpson Tyerman retired to Penlee. Although little-known in Cornwall, he was a noted man in the horticultural world, having held responsible positions at Kew and later as the curator of the Liverpool Botanical Gardens. His best-known work in Cornwall was his design for Kimberley Park at Falmouth.

The property became a nursing home in about 1987, after the death of Mr K.O. Parsons.

The Oddfellows' Hall

The hall, now demolished, was located at the rear of the King's Arms Public House. It was accessed by a doorway off Fore Street, which is now number 54. The first mention of the Hall was in the 1878 Harrod's Directory. The room was rented out for social events and in the late 1890s it was also used as a Men's Institute and Reading Room. For a number of years it

Fore Street, Tregony, from a postcard dated 26 Sept 1904. The shop on the far right was Tonkin's grocery shop. The man on the right is standing outside of the entrance to the Oddfellows' Hall. The lady on the right was Mrs Ellen Snell.

became the venue for the Tregony Petty Sessional Court.

The Loyal St James's Lodge No. 5030, of the Truro District Independent Order of Oddfellows, Manchester Unity, Friendly Society, was formed in a private house at Tregony on

the 21st April 1862. The Society, a type of International Benevolent Society, raised capital by subscriptions, fines, donations and investments, to provide funds for defraying the expenses of its members and their families in times of need (death, illness, unemployment etc). In modern times the welfare state will pay for these needs, but in those times there were no such benefits. The Tregony branch survived until the 1950s before amalgamating with the Truro Branch.

The majority of Tregony's working-class males joined the Oddfellows. The Lodge's records, which are held at the Cornwall Record Office, Truro, provide copious relevant facts for family history research [5].

The cover of an 1886 Rule Book for the St James's Lodge of the Oddfellows.

The Old Rectory

[57, Fore Street]

The architecture suggests that this building was originally a large town house constructed in the late 18th century as a gentleman's dwelling. The first evidence of its existence can be found on the 1787 Basset map of the Tregony Borough, where it is named, 'Yeoman's House'.

The 1841 and 1851 Census Returns showed that Henry Jewell, surgeon, and his family resided there. From 1871 to 1901, the survey revealed that the dwelling was used as a recto-

The Old Rectory, Fore Street, Tregony. Taken from a postcard dated 1904. It was written by some-one in the picture and sent to Mrs Cocks, Ship Inn, Portloe. – "I am sending my photo, can you see me there? Goodbye from N.P.". The Peter Bray Collection

ry and the Rev. John Reid, followed by the Rev. John F. Reeves, inhabited the premises. It is probable that the house was used for this purpose up until 1911 and after that it became the property of Mr Channon, the local veterinary surgeon.

The Royal Cornwall Gazette on the 9th November 1911, reported, 'As there is no Rectory House attached to the benefice of Tregoney with Cuby, the new Rector, the Rev. P.E. Browne, has had to take a house in the Village which is most unsuitable for a Rector of the Parish'.

From 1919 until the 1960s the premises took on a completely different role when they became a centre for agricultural and farming co-operatives, which supplied seeds, animal feed, building material and later coal etc, to the district. The initial owners the Tregony &

District Farmers Ltd, were succeeded by Messrs Hosken Trevithick Polkinhorn & Co who in turn were bought out by Farm Industries Ltd. The house accommodated the branch manager and family as well as also serving as offices. The extensive outbuildings at the rear were designated as warehouses and stores.

Although it has been suggested that this rather grand house may have in the past, when the Borough was in being, been used as either the Town Hall or the Mayor's House, I have never found evidence to support such theories. It seems most unlikely to have been a Town Hall, as the Town's previous two Market Houses would have had facilities for such a room.

The Town Clock, Town Hall & Market House

One of Tregony's most notable features, even today, is the old town clock which stands in Fore Street.

The notion that private investors and public bodies can jointly fund public amenities is not a modern phenomenon. In the early 1830s both sources were used to finance the construction of a building 'complex' for the needs of Tregonians, namely a clock tower, a town hall and a market house. They were sited on a public, open space known as the 'Fair Park'.

In 1833, Capt William Wooldridge R.N. is believed to have funded the building of the clock tower in the memory of his late father-in-law [6], the Rev. Richard Gurney [1749-1822],

Tregony circa 1905. The remnants of the old market houses can be seen on each sides of the Town Clock. The building on the right-hand side was being used as a reading room and band room.

who had served as Rector and also a Capitol Burgess and Chief Magistrate of the old Tregony Borough. In 1864 the tower was renovated.

At about this time, (1830s), the Tregony Borough Corporation had built, in a semicircle around the site of the new clock tower, a town hall and two, single-storied, market houses. The erection dates cannot be precisely fixed but it seems logical to assume that the whole complex was constructed simultaneously, particularly as the original Market House building, which had been located in the middle of the road of Fore Street, was demolished between 1828 and 1841[7]. The stone would have been easily recycled to the new, nearby building site.

According to Mr Parsons, the actual clock, which was installed in the tower, had been made in the 18th Century by a local, master clockmaker, Richard Eva. It had a single hand, hourly striking mechanism which required daily hand winding. The date suggests that its former location was in the original Town Hall. In 1961, Mr Parsons found parts of the

The Clock Tower in 1935, decorated for the Silver Jubilee. This shows how the complex had altered since the 1900s. The old market house on the left had been demolished. The buildings on the right and to the rear had been improved. The clock now has two hands. Unknown source

old clock in a pigsty near to Tregony but they were sold for scrap before he could rescue them. Notably, it was marked with the marker's name and dated 1775. A modern, conventional, two-handed clock replaced the old one in the tower in 1928. In 1998, with the aid of a

Millennium grant, the clock was fitted with an electrical winding system and the tower was completely renovated.

Controversy had surrounded the original ownership of the clock and tower even prior to the demise of the Borough Corporation in 1849.

In July 1857, Mr John Dunstone, a local builder, bought the freehold of the Market House, Clock, Clock Tower, Town Hall and the adjoining meadow, for £62 from Henry Jewel, the last Mayor of the Borough – [confirmed by the

Photographed from the garden of Fairpark House (situated behind Tregony Clock). It has been suggested that the three stone pillars were support columns for the arches of one of the Market Houses. The Author 1996

Conveyance] [8]. In December 1861, many of the local inhabitants became enraged when it became known that parts of the clock had been removed in preparation to sending the clock to Australia. The following day, Mr Bawden, the winder, together with a party of local people, went to the tower and removed remnants of the clock for safe-keeping [9]. They believed that the clock and tower belonged to the people and that the Corporation were only custodians with no right to sell them. Eventually after legal consultations, a compromise was reached, and in 1864 the clock and tower were purchased on behalf of the townsfolk for £12.

An article in the Royal Cornwall Gazette, dated 17th June 1864, confirmed that efforts were being made by the townsfolk to raise a sum of £40 to purchase and improve the clock and tower. It was implied that the clock had not been in working order for some time, and had caused much inconvenience. The improvements included the raising of the tower by ten to fifteen feet. Later that year, the clock and clock tower were purchased on behalf of the local people and from 1894 the upkeep and management were vested in the Tregony Parish Council.

The gradual collapse of the Borough Corporation was very obvious even by 1839. Evidence that neither the Town Hall nor the Market House were needed was apparent. Both buildings were included in a public auction of Corporation property in that year. Interestingly neither property was sold.

The Poplars, Fore Street, Tregony – early 1900s. Located opposite the Old Rectory, this house has now been renamed Renford House. The identities of the two people are unknown. In the early 1920s the house was used as the residence for the local Rector.

By 1883 Kelly's Directory stated that 'there is a Market House in the middle of the Town, now disused.' By contrast, the open space of the 'Fair Park' was used for minor fairs and events up until about 1914.

The Town Hall, which was the building immediately behind the Clock, was eventually converted into a private house, known today as 'Fairpark', 59, Fore Street. Of the two market house buildings which had been located on each side of the tower, one was demolished and the other was refurbished and used after the First World War as a Reading Room and Band Room. Since the 1950s it has been adapted for commercial use, and presently houses the 'Tregony (art) Gallery'.

Public Houses

King's Arms. This ancient public house is now the only one that remains in the Village. A plaque on the wall shows a date of 1651. Its history featured greatly in events and incidents. It was sited near to the important seats of power, i.e. the old Town Hall and Market Place. No doubt it was also frequented by the Oddfellows' members after their meetings which were held nearby.

Town Arms. Sometimes referred to as 'Elliott's Town Arms', this public house was situated in the main street, opposite The Square in the Village. It closed in the 1970s and became Kea

The King's Arms Public House, Fore Street, Tregony, circa 1905. Notice the street lamp. The name of the Licensee is given as S. Phillips. The identities of the people shown are unknown.

Elliott's Town Arms Public House, opposite the The Square in Tregony – 1897. The building has been decorated to celebrate the Diamond Jubilee of Queen Victoria. The two Miss Elliotts are standing outside.

C.T.C. HOUSE.

Wines, Spirits, & Cigars.

Bottled Ales & Home Brewed Beer.

Good Family and Tourist Accommodation.

LUNCHEONS & TEAS.

Parties catered for at shortest notice under personal supervision.

Proprietresses :--

M. J. R. & S. B. Elliott.

TELEGRAMS—ELLIOTT, TREGONY.

An advertisement card for the Town Arms – late 1890s

House, a restaurant and guest house. The members of the Elliott family were the proprietors of the premises from the late 1850s up until 1919, when Miss Sarah Harriet Elliott, the remaining daughter, died.

Gregor Arms, Cornelly. Details of this public house can be seen in chapter 13.

Newspaper Items

Royal Cornwall Gazette – 4th July 1895

[Obviously, Tregony's equivalent of a bull in a china shop!]

'On Tuesday an unwelcome visitor entered the Town Arms, Tregony in the person of a bullock, the property of Mr Nicholls. Although it found its way into the bar and thrust its horns amongst various decanters of spirits, it did not partake of the contents of these vessels, and, therefore, did not lose its head, but followed the dictates of its owner, and left the premises like a well behaved beast, without doing the slightest harm, beyond alarming somewhat Misses Elliott, the proprietresses of the establishment'.

The Town Arms sign board. This was the last external board to be displayed prior to the closure of the public house in the 1970s. The Author 1997

Royal Cornwall Gazette – 8th Feb 1912
Tregoney (summary)

Considerable excitement was caused on Sunday, when a large loft full of straw was discovered to be on fire at the rear of the Town Arms Hotel. Nearly every man, woman and child in the village was quickly on the scene and all helped in carrying water to subdue the outbreak. At considerable risk to himself, Mr C. H. Elliott removed a cask of paraffin. Police Sgt

Lower Fore Street, Tregony – early 1900s, looking up from the The Square. Saddler Chenoweth's shop is visible on the far left. Further up the street is the grocer's shop, known these days as The Londis Shop.

Kendall and P.C. Rogers, with a number of helpers worked hard to prevent the fire spreading. In spite of the strong wind, success quickly crowned their efforts. Had it not been for the prompt efforts of the helpers the whole range of buildings, including the inn, would probably have been destroyed.

The Tregony Borough Poor Houses
A relic of the Borough Corporation days, this building still survives and can be seen halfway up Tregony Hill on the right-hand side. Its long, single-storied structure stands on the top of a bank. Probably built in the 1820s, its purpose was to house the poor of the Borough. In 1841, the Tithe Map indicated that there were 13 individual rooms. These days the building has been converted into six privately owned dwellings which are known as Castle View.

A Social Observation of Village Gossip as Reported by the Royal Cornwall Gazette – 4th March 1897.
[The persons' identities have been removed here, although they were included in the original article.]

Elopement at Tregoney
'The usual quiet and peaceful little Village of Tregoney was thrown into considerable excitement on Thursday last, when it became known that a hind [farm employee] named 'X' had eloped with a single woman named 'Y', with whom, it is stated, he has recently been on very familiar terms. 'X', who has for some years lived apart from his wife, has grown-up sons. The woman is possessed of considerable personal attraction. Our correspondent states that several similar events have occurred in the Village during the last few years'.

References

1   Tregony Census Returns 1841 to 1901 – Cornwall Office.
2   Boscawen Charity Minute Books 1860 to 1932 – Cornwall Record Office (X982/1-2).
3   Abstract Title 1829 – Cornwall Record Office (AD317).
4   Notes on Tregony History by Mr K.O. Parsons, 1970s – copy with Author.
5   St James's Lodge of Oddfellows Registers - Cornwall Record Office (DDX594/32-50).

6 Notes on Tregony History by Mr K.O. Parsons, 1970s - copy with Author.

7 Tregony Boro Map 1828 & Tithe Map 1841 – Cornwall Record Office (X2829/2) & (TM227)

8 Conveyance dated 1st July 1857 – with Author

9 Royal Cornwall Gazette dated 13th Dec 1861 – Courtney Library.

Chapter 7

POLITICS

A lthough I was young to take much notice of politics, I have a few memories; my father was a radical, I know, and from what I saw and heard I should imagine that the majority of the Village were Liberals. Cornwall was considered a Liberal stronghold, a Nonconformist County, where the passing of the Free Education Act, and the memories of the hungry forties by some who experienced them, must have had some effect. In many of the homes there would be photographs of Mr Gladstone and of Her Majesty, the Queen Victoria.

The main parliamentary issues were free trade for the Liberals or protection and imperial preference for the Tories. I remember seeing the Liberal member, Mr W.A. McArthur, being towed to the Board School by men with ropes, the horses having been taken out of his carriage, near the Gallery. Both the Tories and Liberals had a Reading Room each in the Village.

As a boy, and with many others, we used to enjoy singing the Party ditties, which were enlightening:-

Electioneering at Tregony approx. 1906. William Alexander McArthur the sitting Liberal M.P. pays a visit. Tregony was a Liberal stronghold. He was a very popular candidate who won the 1906 election.

'Barley bread as black as your hat,
Tatties fried without any fat,
Figgy pudden without any suet,
That's the way the Tories do it.'
[Sung to the tune of 'Pop goes the Weasel']

The ditty chanted by the Liberals was:-
'The land, the land, tis God who gave the land;
The land, the land, the land on which we stand;
We are not downhearted with the ballot in our hand
God gave the land to the people.'
[Sung to the tune of 'Marching through Georgia']

Additional Information

Royal Cornwall Gazette – 7th July 1892

'Mr W.A. McArthur, the Gladstonian candidate, addressed a most enthusiastic meeting at Tregoney on Thursday evening. Rev. J. Thompson presided. Mr McArthur, who was received with loud applause, said he felt sure the Liberals were not going to be beaten by landlords and dissentient Liberals. No landlord had him in his pocket. He could readily vote without being pulled up by some influential supporter and he was not afraid to give his vote in favour of temperance reform (applause). He always felt he could give his vote for the disestablishment of the Church without having to apologise to any section of his supporters, etc. etc'.

Royal Cornwall Gazette – 11th June 1903

'On Monday evening Mr W.A. McArthur, M.P., who was accompanied by Mrs McArthur, addressed a crowded meeting of his constituents in the schoolroom, Tregoney. Mr T.W. Eastbourne presided. Mr McArthur said it was cer-

This photograph was taken only minutes after the first. Mr McArthur has moved to the pavement where he is addressing the crowd. The house of Mr Gerrans (right foreground) appears to have been the local Liberal H.Q.

Tregony circa 1910. A group of local Liberal supporters holding photos of Mr T.C. Robartes, the Liberal candidate. (L-r) Mrs Jane May; Miss Janie Greet; Mrs Lizzie Jane Mannell; Mrs Rhoda Barnicoat; Mrs Mahala Lidgey & son Herbert; Archie Barnicoat; Arthur May (at back); Herbert Lidgey (front) & Theo Snell. In the background can be seen S Lidgey's Boot/Shoe & General Store.

tain that two things would not be passed over until the people of this country had had a chance of expressing their opinions upon them. He meant the Education Act of last year, (hear, hear), and the London Education Bill. He had not advocated passive resistance. He had not seen his way to take that step. The British Parliament was, after all, supreme. The only way to fight the iniquitous Education Act was to see that when the general election came they turned out the people who were capable of passing an Act so monstrously unjust (applause). When the general election came the Nonconformists would let the Government see what it thought of their education policy. He hoped they might look forward to better times, under a better Government, when a reconstructed scheme of education would be passed. He was sure that until in this controversy they got rid of the interest of particular churches and fixed their minds upon the welfare of the children to be trained, they would not arrive at a settlement of the question which would be a credit to the people of England (applause)'.

Royal Cornwall Gazette – 9th January 1908

'Mr William Alexander McArthur who has represented the St Austell Division of Cornwall as a Liberal since 1887, has resigned the seat. A bye-election took place in 1887 when he was introduced to the Liberal Association. In the 1892 election, he retained the seat against the Unionist, Mr John Westlake. In 1900, he beat his Unionist opponent, Mr Richard Garret by 3,151 votes'.

The Death of the Hon. T.C. Robartes

After the resignation of Mr McArthur, the Hon.T.C. Agar-Robartes of Lanhydrock, Bodmin, became the Liberal Candidate and M.P. for the area, yet, sadly in September 1915, he was killed in action whilst fighting in the First World War.

Chapter 8

SCHOOLDAYS

According to Kelly's Directory, the Village School, which was known as a Tregony Board School then, was built in 1877 at a cost of £1,300 to accommodate 165 scholars. I commenced schooling in 1891 and left in 1898 at the age of 12. At the time I was attending there would be 130 to 140 pupils, grouped in seven standards with three teachers: Mr R.J. Real, Headmaster, and two women teachers, Miss Phillips and Miss Fanny Beard. Fanny Beard, who later married Mr Frank Miners, was the mother of Cecil Miners, Tregony's present Church organist.

The Tregony Board School register shows I entered school at the age of 5 and for this my parents paid a penny a week.

We were summoned into School by a big bell and the morning started with prayers. Each of the two classrooms then had terraced seating: that is, wooden benches built up with steps at one end to enter your place. Miss Beard was my first teacher of the three 'R's'. I also learned to knit and produced two red cuffs to protect my wrists in cold weather. Lessons at the top were composition, essays and learning decimals and on Wednesday

Tregoney Board SCHOOL.
(ESTABLISHED May 6. 1878)

MASTERS OR MISTRESSES FROM THE COMMENCEMENT OF THE SCHOOL.

Name.	Took Charge of School. (Date.)	Left. (Date.)
Geo. D. Millwood	May 6th 1878.	July 11th 1884.
Charles W. Harris	July 14th 1884	May 17th 885
Elizabeth Harris	do.	
Geo. A. Fairbrother	May 18th 1885.	
Enos. Shaw		
E. W. Harding	April 1st 1889	
M. Harding	do	
W. J. Real	September 30/91	Nov 17th 1922
A. Moore	November 20th 1922	

LONDON:
BEMROSE & SONS, 10, PATERNOSTER BUILDINGS; AND IRONGATE, DERBY.

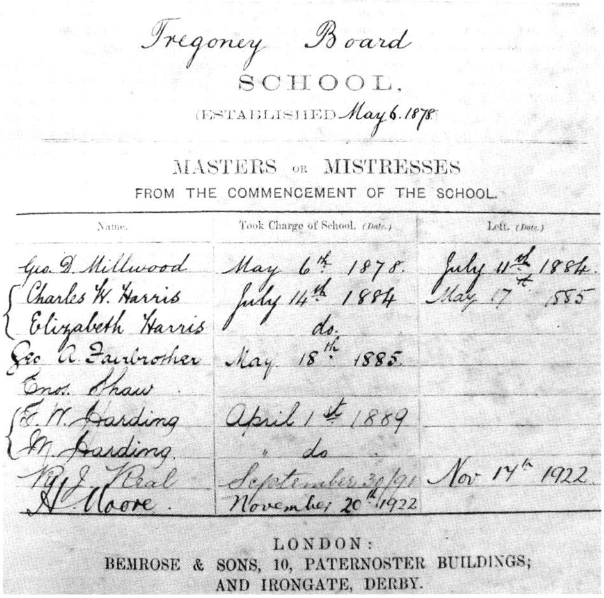

Tregony Board School 1878-1922, list of Headmasters, copied from the school admissions register. Tregony C.P. School – The Author 2001

Tregony Village School – 1978. The headmaster's house was situated on the left-hand side. The remainder of the building consisted of classrooms. School Centenary leaflet

afternoon, drawing for the boys and needlework for the girls. We had no piano, but learned our singing scales from a modulator and then by Tonic-So-Fa chalked on the blackboard in treble and alto, of course. The master gave us the key by tuning fork. Most of our lessons in the Infants and Juniors were by slates and pencils. The Seniors had cards, books, essays, etc. We were graded once a year by one or two Inspectors. I was promoted and remained at the top until I left.

We had two weeks holiday at Christmas, one at Whitsun and four in the Summer. Many boys then went harvesting to earn money to buy new clothes when returning to school, as most would be in rags by then. Children going to school then had no welfare services provided, no medical or dental inspection, or school meals, gym or woodworking equipment, etc. Boys would usually be dressed in corduroy suits and had only one pair of hob-nailed boots. The girls wore printed aprons, their hair long and

THE

LOG   BOOK,

(To be kept by the principal Teacher.)

of the
Tregony Board

SCHOOL.

NEW EDITION.

LONDON:
JAMES MARTIN, 9, LISSON GROVE, MARYLEBONE, N.W.;
G. J. STEVENSON, 54, PATERNOSTER ROW, E.C.
1869

The cover page of the Board School Log Books 1885 - 1921

Tregony Board School, from a postcard dated 1903. The man with the horse and cart is Jo Chenoweth. The gent leaning against the wall is William Gerrans (builder & carpenter) who lived just opposite the school.

occasionally traced and tied with ribbon. After school time, most had some little job of work to do.

The School would be closed for many weeks in some Winters because of measles, scarlatina or whooping cough. The main room was heated by a large Tortoise stove, and the infants class by a smaller stove, but on cold winter days to keep warm, we used to march around the school stamping our feet and singing our marching song, 'Strike up the music and wave high the banner'. There was no water to wash, although two old basins were in the boys' porch. The earth closets (toilets) for both sexes were at the end of the playground and the Headmaster's in his adjoining garden.

Just before Christmas each year, the school gave a Grand concert [with sketches and tableaux] or a pantomime, such as Cinderella, produced by the Headmaster, which was really the big show of the year. Mr Real, the Headmaster, was exceptionally good at this and he

Tregony Fore Street as viewed in a postcard dated 1903. People casually posing for a Joseph Greet photo. At one time the photographer lived in the large house located just above the school.

99

An early 1920s shot looking down Fore Street. The 1917-18 school extension can be clearly seen. It now encroaches as far as the pavement. This photo gives a clear view of the Headmaster's house. Source unknown

had a theatrical friend, Mr Clark, who often assisted. It was held in the school and had to be given on two successive evenings to accommodate the large audiences of parents and friends. We did some training in school but also had to go in the evenings to learn and rehearse our parts.

Whilst I was at school, physical jerks were introduced and some elderly folk said it was wasting time.

Looking back on schooldays, one never sees the same games, with the exception of cricket and football, played today. Enjoyed then were marbles, hoops, tops, rounders, walking on stilts and many others. All these could be played in the street free of all danger of traffic by both boys and girls.

A Tregony School group taken on the occasion of the Coronation of Edward VII in 1902. Many of the pupils are wearing special commemorative medals. The only identifiable persons are Winifred Burley, (far left); and Mr Real, (headmaster). A few locals have also joined the group, including Moses Barnicoat (on the cart).

On leaving school at 12 or 14, all had to find a job of work. A few boys were apprenticed to trades, but the majority on the land, or to some other occupation away from home. The girls, if not required at home, went in domestic service in the Village, on farms or into Truro, where there were more places. The wages, as general servants, were about £8 per year, living in. One old lady tells me she started at £6 per year. They had one afternoon and an evening off in the week and on Sundays, mostly after dinner; so if living in Truro, they could not come home very often, as there was no public transport, save the horse buses, and they were lucky if they could get home once a quarter. The weekend they would not miss would be Feast Week.

Tregony circa 1916. (Front, l-r) Mr R.J. Real, headmaster; Miss N. Chenoweth. (Rear, l-r) Miss Flo Greet; Miss Blake? (Miss Chenoweth spent her entire career at Tregony School. Also she was a Methodist Sunday School teacher for many years).

Tregony Infants class of 1908/9. 1 Mona Lovell, 2 Bert Towsey, 3 William Hosken, 4 Cecil Miners, 5 Cecil May, 6 Les Bennett, 7 May Grigg, 8 Myra Rounsevell, 9 Malvena Dowrick, 10 Archie Dowrick, 11 Wesley Lidgey, 12 Eddie Bazley, 13 Jo Grose, 14 Nicholas Robins, 15 Sid Beard, 16 Frederick Robins, 17 Worrall Trethowan, 18 Miss Blake, 19 Daisy Grose, 20 Mary Greet, 21 Bertha Williams, 22 u/k, 23 Stan Dowrick, 24 Daisy Williams, 25 Winnie Lidgey, 26 Ilene Gay, 27 Vera Evans, 28 Annie Henwood, 29 Carrie Carbis, 30 Elsie Short, 31 Ethel Henwood, 32 Eleanor Philp, 33 Ivy Clemo.

Another group that was obviously photographed on the same occasion in 1902. On the far left is Miss Netta Chenoweth. She attended the school and then became a pupil teacher before training as a full teacher.

Tregony School Class, circa 1918.
(Back, l-r) George Beard, Alfie Wheeler, Virgil Rounsevell, Noel Rounsevell, Fred Roberts and Bill Julian. (Centre, l-r) Lilly Parsons, Mabyn Greet, Pearle Beard, Mahala Barnicoat, Olive Bilkey, Kath Carsons, Amy Davis, Cora Short and Nellie Blackburn.
(Front, l-r) Arnold Barnicoat, Owen Lidgey, u/k, u/k, Stanley Clemo.

At the time of the Hart House fire, there was also a High School for girls at Cuby House, run by a Miss Morgan. A small number of pupils were boarders, the rest were day pupils, being the daughters of farmers or businessmen. This school too, soon closed. A similar one, but much smaller followed in the Village, carried on by a Miss Kirkham, but that did not last long either.

It was about that time that the Village lamps ceased to be lighted, so for a time at least all the 'lights' of the Village seemed to be extinguished!

Additional Information

In the early days of the Board School, small fees [1] were required from parents who could afford them, to pay for their children's education. The rates varied according to the 'standard' or class number in which the pupils were placed. For example, standards 1, 2 and 3 cost one penny per week; standards 4 and 5 – two pence, while standard 6 required three pence per week. Conditions conducive to good learning were almost unobtainable. Imagine 160 pupils, ranging in ages from 3½ to 13 years being taught in two classrooms.

Tregony School Girls' Square Dance Group circa 1921.
(Back, l-r) Norma Brandon & Muriel Julyan; Mahala Barnicoat & Lilly Parsons; Margery Ashford & Winnie Burley.
(Centre, l-r) Daisy Beard & Lidia Kent; Ruby Towsey & Mary Davis.
(Front, l-r) Mabyn Greet & Phylis Clemo.

Tregony School, early 1920s – Empire Day. A typical display when pupils represented the Nations of the British Empire paying homage to Britannia. (Tableau Vivant – a representation of a scene by persons posing silently and motionless).

The School at Tregony remained a 'Board School' until 1902 when a new Education Act passed the control of the education to the Cornwall County Council. The School was renamed the Tregony 'Council School'. With the passing of the 1944 Education Act, the school became known as the Tregony 'County Primary School' and continued as an all age establishment [2]. Tregony County Secondary School opened in 1962. Thereby pupils of 11 years and older, transferred to the new 'top school'.

In 1917/18 alterations were made to the structure of the original building. The terraced seating was removed from the classrooms and an addition was made to the east end when a wing was extended out to the boundary of the pavement.

The Tregony School Log Books for the years 1870 to 1932 still exist (Cornwall Record Office) [3] and coupled with Mr Frank Greet's account of his schooldays they provide interesting social observations. One of the main recurring problems was the terrible school attendance record. Much was unavoidable, because of exposure to bad weather or high rates of illness and disease. Official closures of the school by the medical authorities were not uncommon. A far more prevalent reason for non-attendance was the parents' decision to keep children away from school for work purposes or social events. Here are a number of examples from the Log:

Weather
16th March 1891 – 'The school was closed for the whole week owing to stormy weather. The roads being impassable. The snow in many places, completely blocking them up'.

Illness
13th January 1897 – 'Received Notice from Dr Bonar this morning to close school at once on account of prevalence of measles. School reopened on 2 Feb 1897 but very bad attendance'.

3rd December 1900 – 'Closed school this morning by medical authority, owing to several cases of scarlet fever in the neighbourhood. School reopened on the 14 Jan 1901'.

3rd May 1903 – 'Miss Daisy Gerrans (pupil teacher) died of consumption'.

11th October 1905 – 'Closed school this afternoon by medical authorities owing to an outbreak of scarlatina. 3 Nov 1905 school closure extended again. Reopened on the 27 Nov 1905'.

23rd July 1909 –'Very bad attendance owing to the measles, over 40 cases. School closed on Doctor's orders. School reopened on 20 Aug 1909'.

8th February 1915 – 'School closed for 2 weeks by Dr Bonar owing to the prevalence of whooping cough and influenza'.

Farm work

11th August 1890 – 'Some children are attending very irregularly just now, being kept home by parents to help in the fields'.

17th August 1894 – 'Attendance has been bad all week, owing to so many children being kept home to carry dinners to their fathers engaged in the harvest fields'.

22nd March 1895 –'"Very bad attendance all week, owing to so many of the children being kept at home to work in the potato fields'.

29th October 1897 – 'Several boys absent during the week, being engaged by farmers of the neighbourhood to work in the fields about mangolds'.

15th September 1902 – 'Reopened school today (after 4 weeks of Harvest Holidays), fair attendance, although some boys are still engaged about this harvest'.

Social Events

Either whole day or half day holidays were always given for the following local events: the Tregony Feast; the July Fair; Sunday School Tea Treats of each of the four denominational places of worship; the Band of Hope Fete; Veryan Garden Show, etc. Added to this were the individual events, such as, royal occasions, the Relief of Ladysmith (Boer War), the Truro Music Festival and visits to the travelling Wombell's Menagerie, etc.

Furthermore, the School premises were sometimes closed for events to take place in the classrooms. The rooms were hired out as the venues for polling stations at both local and national elections, the Court House, for fetes and public meetings, etc.

Miscellaneous Problems

The Log Books also highlighted minor, internal, topical incidents. For instance, in early Oct 1889 a verbal confrontation took place between the Headmaster and one of the teachers, Miss Fanny Beard. She had refused the master's request to temporarily take charge of Standards 2 and 3. She was reported for insubordination to the Board. She complained that the master interfered with her work and, rather than submit to interference, she would resign. The Board accepted her resignation. It was evident that internal 'negotiations' ensued, as on the 8th November 1889 'the Board decided to allow Fanny Beard to continue as a teacher and to increase her salary'. Interestingly, the Headmaster resigned soon afterwards!

10th May 1890 – The following was recorded: 'Some of the parents are giving trouble by keeping their girls at home every sewing afternoon because they are not allowed to do any little bits of sewing the parents see fit to send. These parents do not seem to see that needlework has to be taught like any other subject'.

5th November 1890 – 'A boy named W.J.R. (full identity withheld), who only recently returned to school on Monday, after being away since January, was sent home, he having dishonestly taken an exercise book from the school cupboard. A note explaining the matter was sent to the boy's father. The boy to return to school after receiving his punishment, if his parents so desire it,.

Newspaper Items

Royal Cornwall Gazette – 16th December 1897
Miss Kirkham's School

'Seldom has an entertainment been so well supported in Tregoney as that which was given on Tuesday 7th instant; at the Oddfellow's Hall by Miss Kirkham and her pupils. It consisted of songs, musical drills, recitations, dialogues, pianoforte trios, duets and solos. The outburst of merriment created by the dialogue, entitled "That Dreadful Cousin", makes it altogether impossible to pass over without special reference. Miss Kerham's rendering of the song "Bubble" and "The Songs the Children Sing" was highly appreciated, while the rendering of "List to the Convent Bells'" by Misses Kirkham and Buckingham, was enthusiastically encored'.

[Miss Kirkham held School in The Poplars, this house has now been renamed Renford House.]

Royal Cornwall Gazette – 25th April 1912
Tregoney School

'An address on patriotism was delivered at the Council School on St George's Day by the headmaster, Mr Real, and essay lessons on the same subject were written by the scholars. Several patriotic songs were sung and the children saluted the Union Jack'.

Royal Cornwall Gazette – 27th March 1913

'The Tregony Boy Scouts won the prizes presented by Mr G.H. Johnstone at Trewithen on Monday for smartness in attack and carrying despatches. They also won the football match against Trewithan contingent. Sergt Leath [Army] of Tregoney has kindly undertaken the drilling of the Tregoney patrols'.

Further Steps In Education

The old Village School has been converted into a private dwelling. New premises were constructed behind the Parish Church to house the school, providing extra space and modern facilities.

On the 8th September 1993, teachers, parents and pupils, headed by the Headmaster, Mr Paul Rowling, left the old building and walked in procession to the new school. Thereby ending 116 years of local educational history.

Leaving Day – 8th Sept 1993. Children, staff and parents leave the old School for the last time en route to the new building. Supervising is Mr Paul Rowling, the headmaster. The 'for sale' sign is already in place. Source Mr William Barnicoat

References

1 'The Story of Tregony Village School' by Tregony W.I. 1976 – locally distributed booklet.

2 Tregony County Primary School Centenary Souvenir Programme 1978 – copy with Author.

3 Tregony Board School Log Books 1887 to 1921 – Cornwall Record Office (SR/TREG/1-2).

Chapter 9

HIGH DAYS & HOLIDAYS

High days and holidays were few and, apart from Christmas, the two big events were:-

1   The Mazzard Fair (Black Cherry) or the Hiring Fair in July and

2   The Feast, the main event of the year, commencing on the nearest Sunday to the 29th of September. Great preparations were made for the occasion by the housewives and the old Town Oven did much extra baking for the real time of feasting.

All the uncles and aunts and cousins made their way home for the celebrations, some children having to sleep on the floor to accommodate their relatives.

Tregony Feast Week parade of the Oddfellows – early 1900s. Gathering outside the Town Arms in readiness to march to the Church.

The Oddfellows' parade moves off from outside the Town Arms.

Following the Feast Sunday Service in the churches, Monday was the great day. It commenced at 11 a.m. with a parade of the St James Oddfellows Lodge members, meeting on The Square for a service in the Parish Church and led by the Tregony Brass Band, the number would be about 50, dressed in their silk regalia and led by the two Grand Masters, carrying their swords. These were crossed at the head of the Church steps as members marched into Church. In addition to the regalia, the Lodge had two large silk Banners, which must have cost quite a bit in those days. After the dinner, with the usual wine, speeches and toasts, a programme of sports: horse-racing and steeple-chasing took place at Penpel Farm, before ending the evening with the Flora Dance and Fun Fair in the street where young and old made merry. There would also be the usual side-shows, swing boats and probably a penny peep show in a little wooden hut with peep-holes and little lights at the back to show the pictures. What they saw can be seen any day now in a glossy magazine.

About 7.30 p.m. the Band would appear, all merry and bright for the Dance in which young and old would take part and finish up with treating the ladies to a 'Faring' which was expected and enjoyed by all the girls and the married ladies too. A 'Faring' was known as comforts and ginger-breads. This custom has now ceased, but it was general at all Fairs and Feasts throughout Cornwall in those days.

Tregony circa 1910, the parade is passing the Village School en route to the Parish Church.

Tregony circa 1912. Photographed at the top of Fore Street as the parade passes Pine Cotage. The three men leading are, (l-r) Mr A.J. Lovell, Mr Will Evans and Mr Greet.

There would be many standings or stalls to liven the place with the old-fashioned hanging flare lamps providing the lighting. The younger generation would be enjoying themselves in a confetti battle or with teasers! A 'teaser' was a little tube costing 2d filled with about half a cup of water and in great demand by the youngsters who moved around the crowd and gave a little squirt in your ear or on the back of your neck and sometimes even in the face. It was fun at the time but looking back it was rather a dirty game; however, it was as the Poet said, I suppose, 'Other days, other ways, dear me'.

A close-up of one of the silk banners of the St James's Lodge of the Oddfellows. The Author 2004

Feast Tuesday was a much quieter day, although it was kept up, and in the afternoon there were wrestling matches or athletics. The evening programme would be the same as on Monday, but much quieter, for I guess that by that time, all pockets were empty or nearly so.

The July Fair was on a much smaller scale but generally sports, flora danc-

Early 1900s. The Lodge parades in the road outside of the Parish Church, prior to entering the Church for the annual service.

Taken from a postcard dated 1913. Passing Ashby Villa, the parade led by Tregony Band, is returning from the church service.

Aprox 1912, the tail end of the procession as it passes Lidgey's Shop and Coronation Terrace. In the foreground, one of the Oddfellow officials is shouldering a ceremonial cutlass.

ing etc was held with the usual side shows livened by the Village Band and the funfair at night. In the earlier days it was known as a Cattle and Hiring Fair, which meant the farmers and men from long distance met to contract for the harvest month's labour. The men would come prepared to ride back with the farmer where they would live and work for a month. Free beer was also included in their keep.

Because there was no other suitable venue, the Village School was always used for all the big indoor events in the Village, on a stage erected by Mr William Gerrans, the

The Fun Fair at Tregony, early 1900s. Gerran's Ope [now known as Penlee Close] is the location of the fair. The gent with the high hat is probably Richard Beard, father to Lewis and Fred.

carpenter, who lived opposite. Concerts or meetings of a minor character would be held in the Oddfellows Hall adjoining the King's Arms. Entertainments were very frequently given by local artists, comprising sketches, Cornish readings, duets and the comic singer of the day, Charlie Beard, with Mr Real, the Headmaster as accompanist. To advertise concerts, our Town Crier, 'Mr Snell, would make it known by voice and bell'.

Additional Information

Newspaper Reports of Events

Royal Cornwall Gazette - 1st July 1887
Queen Victoria's Golden Jubilee Events – Tregoney

'The festivities here were of a most harmonious and united character. At 11 a.m. a cricket match – Hart House v Tregoney – was commenced and resulted in a tie. At 2.45 p.m. a procession, headed by the Tregoney Brass Band, paraded the street, reaching the Parish Church at 3.30 p.m. A special thanksgiving service was conducted by the Rev J.F. Reeves, the lesson being read by Mr H.J.K. Thompson, and the choral part led by the united choirs of the Village. Re-forming, the procession again proceeded through the gaily decorated streets to an enclosure, where high tea was provided for every inhabitant of Cuby, Cornelly, Tregoney and part

The Stilt Man – Tregony early 1900s. Part of a travelling entertainment group, who regularly visited the Village. Apparently the young children were terrified of him. Photographed outside of Bennetts' grocery shop at the entrance to Stanbury Row.

of Veryan. After tea a series of athletic contests for prizes, provided from Jubilee funds, took place in Lamparrow fields, kindly lent by Mr James Treffry. At 10 p.m. athletes and spectators adjourned to an elevated field, lent by Mr Hosking, and lighted a huge bonfire; subsequently returning to Tregoney to witness the ascent of balloons, rockets, etc. So terminated the enjoyable fête remembered by the oldest inhabitant. To the admirable arrangements of the Rev J.F. Reeves and Messrs H.J.K. Thompson and James Treffry, respectively chairman, secretary and treasurer, is mainly due the entire success of the day'.

A band [possibly not the Tregony Band], leads a procession into the top gate of Penlee House for an event.

The grounds of Penlee House, Tregony, circa 1905. Part of the Feast Week celebrations. Tregony Band is in attendance.

Penlee House, early 1900s. This stall appears to be set up for a 'bring & buy sale', possibly at a fete or fund raising effort.

Royal Cornwall Gazette – 11th October 1894
Tregony Feast

'The above feast was held on Monday, 1st October when the Oddfellows' Club turned out in their usual good style, formed a procession numbering upwards of 150, and, headed by Truro Artillery Band, marched to the Church where the service was conducted and an excellent sermon preached by the Rev J.F. Reeves to a crowded congregation. The Club, after partaking of refreshments, again formed a procession and marched to the field where an excellent programme of sports awaited them and, being attended with fine weather and good management, general satisfaction was freely expressed by those present which numbered upwards of 1200.

The following are the results:

Boys race not over 12 years – Tippett.

One Mile Refreshment Race for Men (a novelty race which caused great amusement as the competitors in the middle of the race had each to eat 1lb of bread and drink a ginger ale). Won by Tippett, a brother to the last winner.

Mens Hurdles – Tippett.

1 Mile Bicycle Race (on grass) - Fred Brenton.

Donkey Chariot Race – won by a fine looking creature owned by Nettle of St Austell.

Ridden Donkey – Kitto took 1st place.

Tregony 1918-19. A fete or tea-treat at Penlee House, Tregony. The ladies standing at the far end of the table are: Emily Blackler [left] and Thamsin Ford [right]. The soldier is believed to be Farrier Sgt W.J. Roberts.

1903. A chapel or church outing to Pendower beach.
(Back, l-r) Mrs H. Greet; Mrs Bennett; Honor Jacob; Mrs Davey; Miss Flossie Perdoe.
(Mid, l-r) William J. Greet; Absolam Beard; u/k boy; Miss Elizabeth Bennett; Miss Mary G. Bennett;
baby Tommy Grose with his mother, Mrs Martha Grose.
(Front, l-r) Alfie Greet; Renee Greet; Percy Perdoe; Jack Grose; u/k boy; Mrs Lavinia Perdoe; Miss
Elsie Grose; Mahala Barnicoat and Mrs Rhoda Barnicoat.

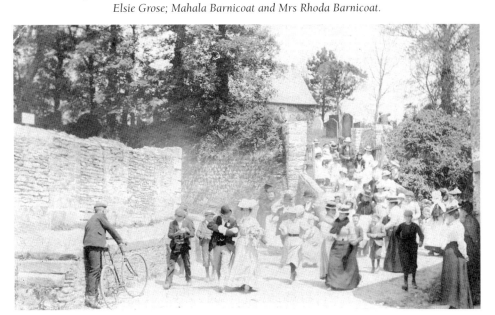

A wedding procession leaving Cuby Parish Church in the early 1900s. [Identities unknown]. The
remnants of the walls of old Hart House School are still visible here.

Then followed a number of races for horses.

Too much cannot be said for the admirable way in which the field was conducted and mention may be made that the refreshments were of a teetotal character, greatly to the comfort of all the ladies and gentlemen who attended'.

King Edward the 7th Coronation – Information

Edward's Coronation was fixed for the 26th of June 1902, but on the 24th, amid general consternation, the king was announced to be suffering from peritonitis, necessitating an immediate operation; and so, the Coronation, for which unprecedented preparations had been made, had to be postponed. The operation was so marvellously successful, and the king's recovery so rapid that within a fortnight he was pronounced out of danger, and soon afterwards it was decided to hold the Coronation service on August 9th. The following is a Royal Cornwall Gazette *report, dated 3 July 1902, which describes the Tregony & District scene on the day of the cancelled Coronation Day, 'Coronation Day was spent very quietly in harmony with the sad circumstances. There were well-attended intercession services at the Parish Churches of Cornelly and Tregony. On Friday the provisions which could not be kept were partaken of. The Fair Park was kindly lent by Mr S. Stephens and at six o'clock about 500 sat down to high tea. Tregony Band played the National Anthem and other suitable music. After the tea a short intercessory service was held and some of the young people enjoyed themselves in games etc., while portions of food were sent to many unable to be present. Great thanks are due to the General Committee whose kind and careful exertions brought about so pleasant a gathering. The funds in hand for sports, carnival, fireworks and bonfire will be held over for the actual Coronation Day'.*

Royal Cornwall Gazette – 3rd October 1907 (extract)
Tregoney Feast – Oddfellows Fete

'Tregony Feast commenced on Sunday when the St James' Lodge of Oddfellows made their annual appeal on behalf of the Royal Cornwall Infirmary. The members paraded the town, headed by Tregoney Brass and Reed Band, under Mr Buckingham and attended service at the Parish Church. Brother Canon Raffles-Flint preached an appropriate sermon and the collection raised £2.12s.

On Monday St James' Lodge held their fete and demonstration. Assembling at the Lodge room at eleven, the members, wearing the regalia, paraded the town and attended service at the Parish Church. Brother J.F. Reeves (Rector) preached from the text, "What is your life?" Dinner was served at the Town Arms at noon, the Misses Elliott putting on a capital spread. The following toasts were honoured:- The Loyal Toast, Ministers of All Denominations, The Army and the Navy, Truro and District Oddfellows, and each was responded to.

118

In the afternoon sports were held which included the following events: open pony race; pebble pick for ponies (confined to within 3 miles); mile flat race for men; high jump; hat, coat & waistcoat race; race for boys; putting the weight; tug-of-war; and the half mile flat race. At half-past seven a Grand Carnival with band and torch lights, paraded the town and prizes were awarded for the following: decorated bicycle and rider; decorated pony, driven; comic character riding; comic character walking; and the decorated donkey'.

Royal Cornwall Gazette – 30th September 1909
Tregony Horse Show

'The first horse show was held at Tregony on Tuesday and attracted an entry of 60, including some of the best animals in the County.

Awards Winners:

Cart or Agricultural Horses - William James of Grampound Road.

Hacks - not exceeding 8 years old, to be ridden - W.H. Yeo of Stonehouse.

Hunters – n/e 8 years old, to be ridden – W.H. Yeo of Stonehouse.

Hacks, Hunters or Harness – n/e 3 years – H.Olds of Tregony.

Flat Races for Ponies, about 2 miles – Monty Best of St Dennis.

Champion Harness Class – any height or age – to be driven in single harness – J. Williams of St Mawes.

Best Jumper – exceeding 15 hands, any age to be tested over banks, imitation walls and hurdles – Jacob Olver of St Stephens.

Harness Horses – any height or age, to be driven in single harness that have never won a prize valued £2 and upwards – W.H. Yeo.

Best Jumper n/e 15 hands, any age – equal Thomas Roberts & H.H. Bishop.

Flat Race Horses, any height, about 2 miles – Monty Best.

Special Prize for Jumping presented by Mr A. Chenoweth to J. Olver of St Stephens.

In the evening a carnival was held and prizes awarded for the following:

Best Character representation, Novel Turnout or Trade Turnout – equal first – E.W. Tonkin and R. Goldsworthy.

Best Decorated Vehicle – equal first – E.W. Tonkin and R. Goldsworthy.

Best Character on Horseback – R. Beard.

Best Decorated Bicycle and Rider in Character – Leonard Real.

Best Comic Character – H. May.

After the show there was a high tea at the King's Arms Hotel, Mr G.W Thomson presiding. Speeches were given by the Judges and others and the catering arrangements were admirably carried out by Mr and Mrs Bazley'.

In Nov 1906, John Coad of Ruan Lanihorne and Florence Buckingham of Tregony, were married at Cuby Parish Church. This photo was taken after the ceremony at the home of the bride's father, Mr James Buckingham, opposite the clock tower in Fore Street.

The Coronation of King George the 5th was on the 22nd June 1911.

Details of Tregony's celebratory preparations were recorded in the Royal Cornwall Gazette *on the 1st June 1911. 'The Coronation Committee have at their disposal the sum of about £21 which has been allotted as follows: tea £9; band £3.10s; sports £4; carnival £9; fireworks £2.2;, bonfire and incidental expenses taking up the remainder. The residents are being invited to decorate their houses and prizes are to be offered for the best decorated houses of various rentals. Mr C.W. Thomson is chairman of all committees, Messrs Blight and Lidgey secretaries, Mr Lovell treasurer, Messrs T. Bennetts, J Kemp, Lovell, E.W. Tonkin and F. Penter are appointed to arrange the programme of sports and carnival. At a public meeting on Tuesday it was decided to have an open-air service instead of the united service in the Parish Church as on previous occasions. The children are to be presented with mugs by Mrs Thomson, and Miss Elliott has promised to present them with medals. Mr Bennetto has kindly placed a field at the disposal of the Committee',*

Royal Cornwall Gazette - 10th October 1912
Tregoney Wrestling

'Wrestling matches were held at Tregoney on Thursday. Mr Bayley acted as secretary and Messrs Josiah Beard (Tregoney), H. Ham (St Dennis) and H. Stephens (St Austell) were stick-

lers. [referees]

Amongst the men to go through in the 1st round, W.H. May (Tregoney) who threw G. Parkhurst (Tregoney). After two further rounds, the final results were: 1, J. Hocking (Nanpean); 2, P. Trethewey (St Austell); 3, J. Sleeman (St Austell); and 4th, F. Beard (Tregoney)'.

Royal Cornwall Gazette – 28th July 1920
Tregoney Fair Sports & Carnival – Revived on Saturday

'July Fair Day at Tregoney, formerly known as the Mazzard Fair, and a day on which the farmers from the whole district came to the town to engage men for their harvest, was revived on Saturday last after a lapse of some years and the sports and carnival and other attractions brought together a fairly large crowd. The sports took place in a field lent by Mr E.C. Barnicoat and the carnival was held in the town in the evening. There was a public tea in the field when the tables were presided over by Mesdames Cutler, R. May, S & G Lidgey, R. Bennett, C. Shapcott, Misses E. Leath and Barnicoat. Tregony Victory Band was in attendance and there was dancing in the Old Fair Park, followed by the furry dance through the town at 10 p.m.'

Tregony Band 1903-4. (Back, l-r) Richard J. Burley; Robert Lyndon; Fred Roberts; James Buckingham [bandmaster]; Jo Chenoweth; Arthur Parsons; George Lidgey. (Mid, l-r) Jack Dowrick; -- Beard; Will H. Keast; Epplett Roberts; u/k; --Grose or Herbert Davey? (Front, l-r) Cyril Truscott; Sam Dowrick; Reg Buckingham and Lewis Greet.

Tregony Band 1905. (Back, l-r) George Lidgey; Fred Roberts; Jo Chenoweth; Fred Dowrick; Richard J. Burley; Arthur Parsons; Norman Buckingham and Ernie Julian.
(Mid) James Buckingham, [bandmaster].
(Front, l-r) Epplett Roberts; George Dowrick; George Towsey; Jack Dowrick; Cyril Truscott; Will H. Keast; Bob Lyndon and – Beard.

Tregony Band posing on the steps of St Cuby's Church, circa 1906. They regularly practiced playing and marching in the main street.
(Back, l-r) Bob Lyndon; Fred Roberts; Jo Chenoweth.
(3rd row, l-r) Richard J. Burley; -- Beard; Arthur Parsons and Will H. Keast.
(2nd row, l-r) James Buckingham, bandmaster; u/k man.
(Front, l-r) u/k man; Jack Dowrick; Reg Buckingham; Fred Dowrick; Charley Burley; Epplett Roberts; Hubert Jacobs and Lewis Greet.

The Town Band

The Band was quite small, but they were very good and used to take several engagements, as there were more local events then, such as tea-treats and local sports which were well supported, as every village and chapel had their own day for pleasure; but today, modern transport has changed all that. The members of the Band were:

Bandmaster – Bob Lyndon; players – James Davey, Jack Dowrick, Jack Ford, George Dowrick, Charlie Jacob, Tom Barnicoat, Tommy Allen, Eplet Roberts, Joe Barnicoat and Hubert Jacob the drummer. The Bandsmen had no uniforms, but of course they mostly wore bowler hats. When travelling to engagements they went by brake with two horses. I don't know the fee charged but I'll guess 30/- to £2, (2/6d per man and transport). There were other village bands in the area, namely Grampound and Sticker and each of them would round off their journey home by playing a march.

Additional Information

Newspaper Items

Royal Cornwall Gazette – 4th October 1906

'Tregoney Brass and Reed Band is making rapid progress under the leadership of Mr Buckingham, who is nobly giving the men the

The bandsman's cap worn by Bob [Robert] Lyndon when he played with the Tregony Band in early 1900s. The dark green hat is piped in red. The black peak bears a golden leaf motif. Also shown is the mouthpiece of his euphonium.

benefit of his knowledge and experience as an ex-Army bandmaster (1st East Yorks Regiment). With a fine set of instruments, a good music library, smart uniforms and keen enthusiasm, the band has won the admiration of the residents in the district and should soon earn a name wider afield'.

Royal Cornwall Gazette – 2nd May 1912

'The members of Tregoney Brass and Reed Band have again shown their ready sympathy in time of need. Once a year in connection with the St James Lodge of Oddfellows on Feast Sunday they make their appeal on behalf of the Royal Cornwall Infirmary and on Sunday last they gave a sacred concert in aid of the widows and orphans of the brave men who perished with the sinking of the "Titanic." The Band, under the conductorship of

Tregony Band approx. 1910 in the grounds of Cuby House.
(Back, l-r) Reg Buckingham; Fred Roberts; Fred Dowrick; Richard J. Burley and Norman Buckingham. (Mid, l-r) George Lidgey; u/k man; Mr Buckingham, bandmaster; Will H. Keast; Cyril Truscott and Solli Mountstephens.
(Front, l-r) Bob Lyndon; George Dowrick; Jack Towsey and George Towsey.

Bandmaster Buckingham, played selections in the Town with much impressiveness and the people responded readily to the collections on the route. The hymns, "Nearer my God to Thee", "Eternal Father Strong to Save", and "Peace. Perfect Peace", were rendered with great pathos, perfect blending of instruments and exquisite harmony. The Bandmaster forwarded on Monday last the sum of £3.4s to the Daily Mail Fund on behalf of the Band. The members of the Band have joined the ranks of thousands of such wholehearted sympathisers and are to be congratulated on their noble effort'.

Royal Cornwall Gazette – 15th Jan 1919 – Tregony Band

'We are glad to know that a special effort is to be made to resuscitate the Brass Band and it is hoped that success will attend. 13 former members have been serving in the Forces and we regret to say that three of them have made the supreme sacrifice and four others have been badly wounded, so that the Band merits support from the public. Mr Fred Roberts is Bandmaster, and if Mr Buckingham, by whose able efforts the old Band reached such a state of efficiency, can be induced to again act as instructor, the success of the Band is assured'.

The Royal Cornwall Gazette – 5th February 1919 – Town Band

'The Band has reformed under the title of the "Victory Band" with Mr Welman of Trewarthenick as President, Messrs E.W. Tonkin and F. Roberts, Hon Sec and Treasurer respectively. Mr J. Buckingham, retired Army Bandmaster, has again undertaken the role of instructor and the Band has already nearly 20 members. The first social in aid of the funds will be held on Friday evening'.

Royal Cornwall Gazette – 12th November 1919 – Charitable Effort

'Tregoney Victory Band which has always been ready to give its services in cause of charity, organised a street collection on Saturday for the "Levant Mine Disaster Fund". The band played hymns through the street, halting at intervals and then adjourning to The Square where a short service was conducted by the Rev F.W. King and Mr Brown (of Gorran), who preached for the day at the Wesleyan Chapel. The large gathering sang hymns led by the band, under the conductorship of Mr J. Buckingham. The collection realised £7.10s. in spite of the inclement weather and it is hoped that the sum will be further augmented from those unable to attend'.

Chapter 10

TREGONY PARISH COUNCIL

A public meeting was held on the 31st December 1894 to inaugurate the first Parish Council for Tregony with Mr Alfie Davey in the Chair. Quite naturally it was well attended and officials of the County Council attended to advise the procedure for the election of members, etc. For the post as Clerk of the Council, three tenders were submitted, one for £4.4s, another at £3.10s and the last at £2 per year. The lowest was accepted from Mr E.W. Tonkin, who held the post for 20 years or more. He also held other offices, such as Land Agent, Rent Collector, Secretary of the Football Club, Agent for the Conservative Party, Clerk to the Hugh Boscawen Charity and for many years was the Sanitary Inspector for the Truro Rural District Council. Although £2 per year seemed a small salary for the Clerk, I noticed that the Board School Caretaker, Mrs Nancy Watts, had 6d per night to prepare the schoolroom, light the lights and fires for the meeting.

At the first well-attended meeting for the election of Councillors, 20 nominations were handed in and voting was by a show of hands. Those elected were:

Messrs J. Davey thatcher and landlord of the King's Arms;

Alfred Davey, thatcher;

W. Gerrans, carpenter;

Mr Wenham of Penlee, retired;

Caleb Greet, bus proprietor;

Absalom Beard, smallholder;

William Blight, roadman and local preacher and

James Greet, (my father), gardener and potato merchant.

These were the first Councillors and we have them to thank, even today, for the valuable services they rendered. I suppose these men now they had been given some power, felt they wanted to show some results and it was not long before they required the deeds of the Town Clock to be in their possession. At the time they were held by Dr. Bennett but, after some correspondence, they received them for safe custody. Another thing they did was to write to Mr

Thompson relating to his taking of tolls for the use of The Square by Fairs, etc. He replied that he had owned the Square for 20 years and had no intention of agreeing to the Council's request. However, disagreement of the tolls seems to have soon petered out when Mr Thompson had left the Village after the fire at Hart House School. At this time the Rateable Value of Tregony was reduced by £3 per year as a direct result of the fire closing the school and in 1895, according to the Council there were 38 unoccupied cottages in Tregony and many were in a bad state. A leading Councillor remarked at the time, that, "Tregony was a rapidly declining Village."

War in South Africa Relief Fund – 1899. An official notice regarding the collection of funds at Tregony. £6. 5s. 6d was raised. The full document lists the names of the donors together with the amounts that each had contributed. The Author 2004

Additional Information

Topics Discussed by the Parish Council

St Just Docks & Railway Link
[This scheme to build a large docks and railway connection was proposed on several occasions from the 1830s to 1920s, but was never adopted.][1]

1. Royal Cornwall Gazette – 14th January 1909 'New Scheme for St Just. Plans. It is proposed to build docks on the eastern side of Falmouth Harbour and by constructing a branch railway of about nine miles through the Roseland district to effect a junction with the main line at Grampound Road and thus saving a considerable amount of time and distance. The proposed St Just Docks have been designed to accommodate the largest vessels now afloat. It is proposed to erect three jetties, breakwater and quays together

with sheds and equipment for dealing with passengers, mail and for goods. The breakwater is designed to cope with the berthing, at one time, of three liners, each 500 to 1000 feet long. Trains would be able to come alongside the vessels and passengers, mail, etc be landed or embarked under cover. The docks would be especially equipped for dealing with china clay traffic and the plans provide for a length of quays and berthage of over two miles. At the northern end it is proposed to construct two dry docks of 1000 and 500 feet in length together with engineering and repair works close at hand.

The scheme includes a terminal station and the construction of a branch line of railway of about 13 miles. The line would commence at St Just, passing through the Roseland, transverse the upper reaches of the Fal Valley and join the Great Western main line at a point one and a half miles east of Grampound Road station. Intermediate stations are to be built at Grampound and Philleigh to serve Veryan, Portloe, Tregony, Gerrans and Portscatho. It is suggested that at a later date it might be practicable to further extend this branch up the Fal Valley, with a station at Tregony, to join the mineral railway at Retew and in a northerly direction to effect a junction with the London and South Western Railway at Wadebridge. Apart from the china clay, the engineer estimates that the railway would carry a considerable agricultural traffic as well as attracting a large passenger traffic to St Mawes and Portscatho'.

2. Royal Cornwall Gazette – 17th March 1910 – Parish Council. 'A discussion took place about the St Just Docks (Experimental Works) Bill, at present before Parliament and great indignation was expressed at the actions of the Great Western Railway Co. in opposing the Bill as construction of the docks and connecting railway line would prove an inestimable boon to the district by opening up and developing a tract of agricultural land, considered to be the most fertile in the West of England, and by creating a large touring traffic to the seaside resorts of Gerrans, Portscatho, St Mawes and other favourable spots in the Roseland district, which are at present inaccessible. Resolutions in support of the scheme were unanimously passed and it was decided to write to Mr T.C. Agar-Robartes, M.P. and Mr J.C. Williams, the County Councillor for the Division, asking them to support the scheme'.

3. Royal Cornwall Gazette – 24th December 1918 – Parish Council. 'Plans of the proposed St Just Docks and Railway were discussed and it was unanimously decided to support the scheme in every possible direction as it would be an immeasurable boon to the whole district and county generally'.

4. Royal Cornwall Gazette – 21st December 1921 – 'A communication was read from the Workers' Union asking the Parish Council to do its best to press forward the St Just Ocean Wharves and Railway scheme'.

5. Even up until 1924, the revival of the legal powers were being sought for the possible building of the Port and Railway. Mr Cecil Pearce of Daddiport, Tregony, has in his possession a document that was served on his father in 1924, which gives details of the land that might have been required under compulsory purchase for the proposal. The project never actually got off the ground and nothing more has been heard of the grandiose scheme.

Public Phone Call Office
1. Royal Cornwall Gazette – 7th March 1912 – 'The Council decided to ask the Postmaster General to consider the question of providing a public telephone call office at the Post Office'.

2. Royal Cornwall Gazette – 28th March 1912 – 'The Clerk reported that he had reason to believe that Sir Lewis Molesworth of Trewarthenick would guarantee a large portion, if not the whole, of the amount required by the authorities in respect of the proposed telephone call office at the Post Office, but as he is out of England it would be advisable to await his return before making the application'.

Telegraph Office
Royal Cornwall Gazette - 25th September 1913 – 'The Parish Council have decided to petition the Postmaster General to re-open the telegraph office on Wednesday afternoons'.

Public Roads & Footpath
1. Royal Cornwall Gazette – 7th March 1912 – 'Complaints were received of the condition of Lady Lane and Mill Lane, but the Council had no jurisdiction and no action was taken'.

2. Royal Cornwall Gazette – 26th November 1914 – 'The Chairman said he had informed the County Committee that if the County Council would deal with the question of the flooding of the Ruan and Tregoney road, it would relieve nearly all the unemployment in the district and at the same time make a permanent and much needed improvement. The road was under water for over a quarter of a mile for months at a stretch during the winter months. If the river was cleaned up from Tregoney Bridge to Ruan Sett at a suitable time, the quantity of splendid sand taken out would greatly assist towards defraying the cost. Mr Keast said it was a shame that the County Council had not taken the matter in hand long ago. Their attention had been drawn to it times enough. It was decided to write to the County Council again on this question'.

3. *Royal Cornwall Gazette - 30th November 1916* – *'The low lying portion of Tregoney – Ruan road has been under water to a depth of from one to two and half feet for some weeks and practically impassable. A motor car used by a gentleman buying timber for the Government got into the deep part below Treskerby Wood and had to be dragged out by a horse'.*

4. *Royal Cornwall Gazette – 17th September 1919* – *Mr W.H. May drew attention to overhanging trees at the Old Rectory, Myrtle House and the Bible Christian Chapel, and it was decided that they should be lopped but not as to cause disfigurement'.*

5. *Royal Cornwall Gazette - 25th February 1920* – *'Mr Burley drew attention to the alleged obstruction of the footpath in Cuby Parish and threatened to draw the attention of the District Council to the matter unless the obstruction was removed. It was stated that Cuby Parish Council had called the attention of the owner of the farm to the matter'.*

The Private Well in Well Street

Royal Cornwall Gazette - 25th February 1920 – *'Much Disputed Well. [The well was situated immediately in front of the Old Town Oven] – the Parish Council again considered the question of the locking by Mr John Vindicombe of an alleged public well. The matter had already been discussed on two occasions and also by the Truro Rural District Council, who had before them evidence of some of the oldest inhabitants as to the public having used the well from time immemorial. The Rev F.W. King moved that the Council take no action in the matter. Seconded. Resolution passed'.*

Royal Cornwall Gazette - 30th June 1920 - *Evidence Presented to the Truro R.D.C Committee at Tregony on the Use of Well Street, Well.*

1   Mr Vindicombe, the present owner of house & premises adjoining the well, said he had known it for 7 years and it was a private well and the deeds mentioned the well as belonging to it. (The deeds prior to 1912 were not produced).

2   Mrs Elizabeth Beard, aged 76, stated that her husband, Mr Absalom Beard, formerly owned the property. She had known the well for 40 years and they locked it at times by day and night.

3   Mr Absalom Bennetts, nephew of the late Absalom Beard, corroborated.

4   Mr Arthur Chenoweth said he had known the well for 30 years and had seen it locked at times during the day, but Mr Absalom Beard was a kind man and allowed people to have water there.

5   Mr Josiah Beard deposed to knowing the well about 80 years. He had seen Peter Beard stop boys from dipping dirty pails into the well, but admitted the public had come there and nearly dipped the well out, so there was very little water left for his Uncle and Aunt.

6   Mr Edward Bennetts, aged 81, said he married the daughter of Peter Beard, the father of Absalom Beard, and who owned the property until his decease. Peter Beard never denied anyone from having water, as he knew it was a public well. At first there was no door to the well and the first one was put there by public subscription collected by Joseph Woolcock.

7   Mr John Henry Matthews, a nephew of the late Peter Beard, asserted that the latter had never disputed the right of the public to the well. He (Mr Matthews) contributed towards the first door to the well and stated that persons cleaning out the well were paid by subscriptions from the public using the supply.

8   Mr E.W. Tonkin, for 19 years the Sanitary Inspector to the Rural District and for 17 years the Clerk to the Parish Council, said he had known the well nearly all his life. It was the only public water supply for the centre of the Village until the Coronation Pump was fixed on The Square. He had instructed Mr Absalom Beard to lock the door of the well at night for protection of the public as persons came during the night and sometimes emptied the well. Mr Beard had never claimed to him that it was a private water supply. Until the first door was fixed it was always open to the public and if former owners had any title to the well, they could have shut up the doorway and had a pump inside their premises, where the public could not use it. He claimed that it could be proved that the right of the public to the well by long usage had been established and if it was once a public water supply, it must always be a public water supply.

The Truro Rural District Councillors were of the opinion that the well was a public one (4 April 1920 RCG).

Dangerous Buildings
Royal Cornwall Gazette – 20th April 1911 – 'Complaints were received of the dangerous condition of some old ruins of houses in Gurney Row, Tregoney; also the owners, in trying to protect the same, instead of taking them down, had enclosed half of the roadway in the row with barbed wire. It was decided that the Council should meet on the spot on Monday next, and if necessary, report to the District Council'.

Clock Winding Pay Increase
Royal Cornwall Gazette – 5th October 1916 – 'The caretaker of the Town Clock asked for increased remuneration in consequence of having to stop the clock from striking from 8 p.m. to 7 a.m., as ordered by the Police. It was decided to grant £1 extra and to inform the

Supt. of Police that in future such notices should be served on the Council."

General Nuisances

Royal Cornwall Gazette – 5th October 1916 *– 'Mr A.J. Lovell reported that a certain pig-keeper, residing near Stanbury Well had been dipping dirty pails into the water, and it was decided to draw his attention to the matter'.*

Parish Councillors' Court Case – Disturbance

1. Royal Cornwall Gazette - 2nd May 1912 *- letter from Mr Tonkin wishing to retire as he can no longer put up with the insults from Mr Lovell (a fellow Councillor).*

2. Royal Cornwall Gazette – 20th September 1917 *– Tregony Parish Council – Meeting Breaks Up in Disorder. [A summary and background].*

At about midnight on Saturday, 8th Sept 1917, after a long and fretful meeting of the Parish Council, mainly concerning the accuracy of the minutes of a previous meeting, relating to the Town Clock Deeds, tempers flared and the assembly broke up in disorder. There had been a history of rivalry and distrust between certain of the members and this had

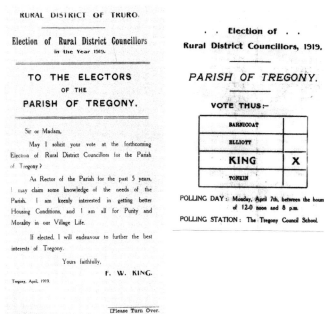

An election advertisement on behalf of the Rev K.W. King, Rector of Tregony. CRO-(P/44/2.1B)

boiled over at the meeting. This acrimony had been much publicised, as each of the members had had their accusations and defences recorded in 'letters to the Editor' (of the Royal Cornwall Gazette), which had been published prior to the fateful meeting.

3. Royal Cornwall Gazette – 24th September 1917 *– Tregoney Petty Sessions – Fighting at the Parish Council – Tregony Town Clock Deeds. [A summary].*

As result of an uproar that had been caused between certain of the Councillors at a Council meeting on Saturday, 8th Sept, charges of assault had been made by several of the council-lors against each other. It had been stressed that no actual blows had been struck but that some pushing and shoving had resulted. After hearing evidence for over two hours, and before it was completed, the Chairman of the bench stated that the Magistrates had heard quite enough and retired to consider the matter. On returning the Chairman said that it was a very silly case arising out of a breezy meeting of the Parish Council and was not the sort of case that should waste the time of the Court. It was quite evident that a technical assault was com-mitted by T and W on L. [identities withheld]. There was hardly any provocation and it was simply because there was no chairman to keep order. They were fined £1 each and the cross summons issued by T would be dismissed. Mr T protested that three of his most important witnesses had not been heard and that he had not had the chance to state his case and it was very unfair. The hearing lasted about two and a half hours and the Court was crowded.

Royal Cornwall Gazette – 22nd October 1919 - Tregony Strike
'Apparently in order to be in fashion, our old Town Clock has gone on strike, or, rather, it has ceased to strike for nearly a week. Whether it went on strike (or off its strike) out of sympa-thy with the caretaker, who threatens to go on strike because the Parish Council would not give him the increase of pay asked for, or whether it is a case of "something wrong with the works", is not clear, but it is hoped it will soon strike the hours again, as, at present, workers do not know what time to cease work'.

Reference

1   Map of the proposed railway line via Tregony 1914 – Cornwall Record Office (AD/28).

Chapter 11

LAW & ORDER

(An additional chapter compiled by Franklin Grigg)

The Police

The first Cornwall Constabulary Police Station in Tregony was located in a terraced house which is now known as 20 Tregony Hill [the property next down from the 'Kea House' guest-house]. Each of the Census Returns from 1861 to 1891 showed a police officer and his family resident at this address. One of the ground floor rooms at the rear had been converted into a cell and evidence of this was visible until relatively recently. In about 1910, the Police Station transferred into other premises at Kenwick House. [This is now known as 18 Fore Street. It is situated opposite the King's Arms Public House. At present it is the Tregony Rectory]. The Sergeant and his family resided there however; there were no facilities for a lock-up. This remained the site of the station until about 1960 when the present Police Station and two houses were built in Cuby Lane. To the older generation this was always known as Conce Lane.

The original Cornwall Constabulary Police Station in Tregony. It was the white house next down from the Town Arms. A 'Police' sign can be seen above the front door. Postcard dated 1908.

133

Kenwick House, 18 Fore Street, Tregony, [centre house]. From about 1910 until 1960 this was the location of the second Cornwall Constabulary Police Station at Tregony. Since about 1998 it has been used as the Tregony Rectory. The Author 2004

This is a 1991 view of the present Tregony Police Station which is situated in Cuby Lane. Pictured are Traffic Warden Terry Spires, (left) and Constable Chris Jellis. The Author

The original Police Station later became the late Mr & Mrs Anthony Wheeler's General Store and the shop closed in 1998. In the 1920s a pair of 'stocks' were found at the back of the premises. These must have been quite ancient because the use of such items had long been banned. The Royal Cornwall Gazette dated 11th October 1861 had a short article titled 'Punishment in the Stocks'. It related the case of a local labourer, named G.B. [full name withheld], who was sentenced by the Tregony Sessions Court to six hours in the stocks for failing to pay his fine for drunkenness in the street. He was arrested by Sgt West and placed in the stocks which were situated in front of the Market House.

Accounts have been told by the older generations of stories passed down to them by their ancestors of the treatment, imposed on local individuals known as the 'insane'. On fine sunny days a 'deranged' person could be brought to The Square and left there, secured by chains. Probably regarded as a kind of 'fresh air therapy' for the poor soul, one wonders what became of them when the weather was not suitable!

The Old Town Jail

This relic of the old Tregony Borough days is still in existence. The building, long since converted into a detached dwelling, is located next down to the Almshouses and is known as 'Castle Cottage', 12 Tregony Hill. According to Dr Bennetts, a 19th century local historian, the jail was built in 1735 and it was used up until 1870. This latter date overlaps neatly with the opening of the Cornwall Constabulary Office at Tregony.

The Old Town Jail [next to the Almshouses]. Built in 1735, it was used up until about 1870. It is now a private house. The Author 1992

The Local Court

To deal with local justice, Tregony had its own Petty Sessions Court which later became known as the South Powder Magistrates' Court [1]. According to the 1889 Kelly's Directory, proceedings were held at the Oddfellows' Hall, Tregony, on the first Monday of every month, commencing at 11 a.m. The Court's jurisdiction covered the areas of Cornelly, Cuby, Gerrans, Lamorran, Merther, Philleigh, Portloe, Portscatho, Probus, Ruan Lanihorne, St Anthony, St Michael Caerhays, St Just, St Mawes, Tregony St James, Tresillian, Trewithian and Veryan.

What a way to come for some poor chap, say, at St Anthony, who had been caught without any lights on his bike; plus, he probably had a fine to pay! On occasions up until about the 1870s, Magistrates also held Court at Ruan Highlanes.

The Justices were drawn from the respected, upper classes and senior clerics of the area. In 1889, the following were listed: The Rev Hon John Townsend Boscawen, Rector of Lamorran – Chairman; James Hendy Esq of Trenoweth, Grampound Road; Joseph Charles Kennerley Esq of The Haven, St Mawes; the Rev Lewis Morgan Peter of Treviles, Ruan Lanihorne; and Thomas Henry Vyvyan of Parc Behan, Veryan.

The Cornwall County Record Office holds the Registers of cases heard and penalties imposed at the Tregony Court from 1892 to 1909. The cases portray some of the social conditions that were prevalent in a rural area at the time. Prosecutions for drunkenness, assault, including domestic violence and neglect, poaching and begging were quite common. The names of several of Tregony's well-known families (my own included) appear in the list of defendants' with some regularity. In 1907 the court venue was moved to the Tregony School Room. Later it was held at the Tregony Church Hall and continued there until about 1984, when the Court was incorporated into a district court at Truro.

The more serious cases [few in number] were committed to the higher, County Quarter Sessions or the Assize Courts. The sentencing power of the local Petty Sessions was restricted, and fines were usual, but imprisonment was not unknown. For instance, it seemed to be common practice for beggars arrested under the Vagrancy Act to be given four weeks detention with hard labour. In 1902, a 'young man' from St Just was ordered to be given six strokes with a birch rod and pay costs for stealing a fowl. Interestingly, quite high percentages of 'not guilty' verdicts were delivered by the Magistrates, and this seemed especially so in domestic cruelty and neglect cases. This fact adequately demonstrates the inequality of gender that was apparent at that time.

Here are a few examples of pertinent articles that were recorded in the local newspapers:

Royal Cornwall Gazette – 1st January 1886 – Letter to the Editor
The Police & the Roughs at Tregony (summary)

'I wish to call the attention of our Magistrates to the behaviour of the young men of this place,

particularly on Saturday evenings after clearing of public houses, when the noise and uproar is dreadful and the language most disgusting. I would therefore beg to ask what is become of those energetic guardians of the peace – the Police? It appears they are never in the way when wanted or in plain words, always manage to keep out of the way. I do not hesitate to say that if some of our old women were as well paid as our resident policeman, they would have recognised some of the lawless young ruffians and brought them to justice.
Signed – a Ratepayer'.

Royal Cornwall Gazette – 15th January 1886 – Letter to the Editor
Tregony: Its Inhabitants and Police (Summary)

'Our one policeman, who is a sergeant of the district, knows his duty and does it, I believe faithfully, in an independent manner, to the satisfaction of all, well disposed inhabitants. The term 'roughs' as applied to the working men is a gross libel. From my experience amongst their class, I have never met with a more civil, industrious, sober or law-abiding people (no doubt there is a black sheep here and there). We have just passed through the unusual excitement of an election and the Christmas festivities, and so far as my own observations go and that of my neighbours, I have not heard of a single case of noise that would justify the Sergeant's interference.
Signed: John Tyerman'.

[There was a reply from the original complainant, to Mr Tyerman, briefly stating – "How would Mr Tyerman know anything about the disturbances as he lives in a large residence which is out of the noise and hubbub of the place and what does he know about black sheep, as he is only at Tregony for a few minutes at a time?"]

Royal Cornwall Gazette – 26th March 1891
Giving a Vagabond The Frog's March

'Thomas Mitch, aged 40, a tramp, was apprehended at Tregony on Thursday by Sgt Box and P.C. Jenkins on a charge of behaving indecently to young females at Tregoney Bridge. On prisoner being apprehended he became very violent, resisted and assaulted both officers and was eventually taken to the Tregony lock-up by a posse of men under frogmarch. On Friday he was brought before Rev A.R. Tomlinson at Truro and was remanded to the next Tregony Petty Sessions'.

Royal Cornwall Gazette – 9th April 1891
Damaged in Helping the Police.

'Mr Stephen Pascoe, of Tregoney, wrote through his solicitor, asking the Police Committee to grant him some compensation for damages sustained whilst assisting P.C. Hall in the execution of his duty at Tregoney some time since. Mr Pascoe was aiding the policeman in conveying a prisoner to the station, when he tripped and hurt his shoulder, being incapacitated from work for some time. Mr W.C. Pendarves said the judge might have awarded some compensation, but he did not think anybody else could do so. Colonel Gilbert (Chief Constable) said he should like to see something awarded to Mr Pascoe, as it might be a help to the police in the future. It was understood that the clerk would ascertain the legal powers of the committee in the matter'.

Royal Cornwall Gazette – 4th April 1901 - Tregoney Petty Session

'Mrs S.M. (identity withheld) of Tregoney applied for a separation order on account of alleged persistent cruelty by her husband. Evidence was given that the parties had been married for nine years and had six children. On March 16th they had a disturbance and the wife stated that her husband took up a chair to strike her. Prior to that date she had not spoken to him for a fortnight. She further alleged that in September last she had been struck in the eye by a boot thrown by him. The husband denied the facts and said that his wife was in the habit of sulking a great deal. The application was refused'.

Royal Cornwall Gazette – 13th June 1907
Cornwall Assize Court – The Tregony Oddfellows Case (Summary)

'X (name withheld), aged 33 yrs, a gardener, was indicted for embezzling and stealing sums of money, amounting to of £129.7s.8d, the property of the St James' Lodge of the Oddfellows, Manchester Unity, Friendly Society, of which he was the secretary at Tregony. He further admitted making false entries in the resolution book and converting certain sums of money for his own use. The discrepancies had come to light after a special audit had been made. In mitigation, the defence solicitor said that the accused had married when he was 19 and now had 7 children. In 1898 his father died leaving 7 children of which 3 were infants. The accused, who had an income never exceeding 15 to 16 shillings a week, undertook the care of his mother and the 3 infants. His situation had been going from bad to worse and was never far from a starvation level. His Lordship remarked that there were circumstances which had to be taken into consideration, the money had not been spent on gambling, but that societies must be protected. He sent the accused to prison for six months with hard labour'.

Royal Cornwall Gazette – 4th May 1911
Tregoney Petty Session – Allegation of Child Neglect (summary)

'J.N. (name withheld), a farm labourer of Fair Cross, Cuby, was summoned for neglecting his five children, whose ages ranged from 5 to 11 years. The prosecution was brought by the

N.S.P.C.C. Evidence was given that on the 6th February, Mr E.W. Tonkin, the Truro Rural District Council Sanitary Inspector, visited the house and found that although structurally fit it was in such a filthy condition as to be injurious to the health of the children. All the rooms were very dirty with cobwebs hanging from the ceilings and walls. Downstairs the only articles of furniture were a table and two broken chairs with a tin box. On the 11th February Inspector Wall (N.S.P.C.C) and Police Sgt Kendall visited the house at 11 a.m. and the defendant was in bed but he bolted into a coal-house where he was found. The only furniture in the bedroom was an iron bedstead with no bedding but dirty rags on it, and the children slept in a corner of the same room on a heap of filthy rags. There was no money in the house and the only food was a small piece of cake and some milk, not sufficient for the family for another meal. The children were not properly nourished and were insufficiently clad. The wife appeared to be cowed down. The defendant admitted that he had given way to drink. He earned 15 shillings per week; the cottage was rent-free, with the usual privileges and that there was plenty for him to do. Mr Wall advised the defendant to work that afternoon and earn some money with which to buy food for the weekend. On the following day, Dr Barry visited the house and found the advice had not been followed and there was absolutely no food in the place. The Doctor kindly relieved the children, who were removed to the Workhouse. The Court was told that the defendant was now in a permanent situation and it was believed he would try to do better and that the case should be adjourned in order that the Society might keep the family under observation. The case was put back for a month'.

[The case was adjourned again for a further month whilst the R.S.P.C.C. monitored the family, but unfortunately, I was not able to find the result of this case.]

Royal Cornwall Gazette – 7th November 1912
Tregoney Petty Session – 'Short Weight'

'Mr H.W. (name withheld) baker of Probus appeared charged with selling bread otherwise than by weight. Police Sergeant Kendall stated that on the 10th October a young man employed by the defendant came to his house selling bread and he asked him for two 2lb loaves. The man told him that he did not sell by weight and the loaves were taken to Mr Robert's shop (local Tregony grocer) and weighed, when it was found that one loaf weighed 1lb 14ozs and the other 1lb 13ozs. On the 17th October the Sergeant again asked for two 2lb loaves, which weighed 1lb 13ozs each. He paid 3d for each of the loaves. The defendant, through his Solicitor, entered a guilty plea to the technical offence but contended that the public got what they paid for. The 3d priced loaves were weighed in dough and there was always shrinkage in the baking. No two came out the same weight. The public had not been defrauded and in fact had received full value for their money. The defendant agreed that the notices

advertising the bread were illegal and had since been withdrawn. The Chairman of the Bench said that the law was for the benefit of the public but as it was regarded as a technical offence the defendant would only be fined one shilling and costs'.

Royal Cornwall Gazette – 9th January 1913
Tregoney Petty Session – Wound the Clock

'J.B., [name withheld] labourer of Tregoney, pleaded not guilty to being drunk and incapable in Fore Street on Sunday. P.C. Sambells stated at 9.45 p.m. he saw the defendant leaning against the wall of a house, hopelessly drunk. He tried to walk away but fell down and at his request the witness assisted him home. The defendant stated that he had only one pint of beer and just before the Constable saw him he mounted the steps of the town clock to wind the clock. He was not drunk. His hat blew off and as his sight was bad from cataracts, he was groping around to find it. Fined one shilling and costs'.

Royal Cornwall Gazette – 17th August 1916
Tregony Petty Session

'A cattle drover, W.M. [identity withheld] of Tregony pleaded "not guilty" to a charge of 'using profane and obscene language on the 14th July'. P.C. Sambells stated that he saw the defendant with a gun in Fore Street and on asking him for his licence, the defendant became abusive. Police Sgt Patrick corroborated and in cross-examination admitted that he referred to the defendant as 'Zulu' [a nickname of the defendant]. The defendant alleged that Sambells did not ask for his licence but said he had no right carrying the rifle and ordered him indoors. He had a licence. He intended to use the rifle for frightening the rooks from his potatoes. He had been to France fighting for his country and the Police had no right to speak to him like they did. The Chairman, Mr W.C. Blamey, said that they were satisfied that bad language was used, but that as the defendant had been provoked, the case would be dismissed'. [Game – all!]

Royal Cornwall Gazette – 7th December 1921
Tregoney Defendant's Wish to Have another Chance

'V.M. [identity withheld] a young labourer of Tregoney appeared before Col Nowell-Usticke and the Magistrates at Tregoney Petty Sessions on Monday and pleaded not guilty to a charge of being drunk and disorderly in Fore Street on Nov 23rd. Police Constable Wadge said just after 10 o'clock at night the defendant was outside the public house shouting and looking for a fight. When someone told him the policeman was nearby, the defendant used bad language and said he did not care for the policeman and fell against the constable. The officer had to take him home, where he (the defendant) shortly after frightened his mother and sister out of the house. The defendant said he could not afford the expense of getting witnesses. He had been suffering from nerves ever since he was inoculated in the army. He asked the Bench to bind him over to give him a chance of turning over a new leaf. In spite of previous convictions and the last fine not having been paid, the Bench agreed to do this, but warned him that if he came there again he would probably go to prison'.

The Coroner's Court

All cases of accidental, sudden or unnatural deaths had to be reported to Her/His Majesty's Coroner. Ascertaining the circumstances surrounding the fatalities was his responsibility, and if necessary, the cause was determined by a Coroner's Court.

In serious cases, a local jury was sworn in to give judgement. The area Coroner for Tregony was based at Truro. It was the task of the police to collect any evidence on behalf of the Coroner. This information together with any medical data obtained from post-mortems or medical histories were presented at the hearing.

Here are few examples of such tragedies that happened in Tregony:

Royal Cornwall Gazette – 17th May 1888 – Boy Drowned

'A sad accident occurred on Thursday afternoon in the Tregony River, by which a little boy named Edwin Tiller, aged three and a half, lost his life. Deceased and some others went to the River and his companions took off their boots and went into the stream, leaving the little one on the bank. By some means he fell into the water and there was a rather strong current running at the time. He was carried away before his companions could reach him. They immediately raised an alarm and attracted the attention of a young man [name withheld]. He was on his way to attend a funeral and, being attired in his best clothes, he did not care to enter the water but went to fetch a bar of iron with which to rescue the drowning boy. In the meantime a blacksmith, named Hugh Eplett Roberts, who was working nearby, hearing what had happened, hurried to the spot, sprang into the river and brought the boy to shore, but not in time to save his life. He had been carried about 300 yards and was quite dead when Roberts picked him up. Mr John Carlyon held an Inquest on the body on Friday, when the jury, of whom Mr David Barnicoat was foreman, returned a verdict of 'Accidental drowning'.

Royal Cornwall Gazette – 19th December 1895
Sad Fatality at Tregoney

'An Inquest was held at Tregoney on Saturday by Mr E. Lawrence Carlyon, relative to the death of Samuel Tregeagle, aged 85 yrs, a retired carpenter, who lived at Tregoney. The evidence showed that at half-past four on Tuesday morning a man named Miners, a neighbour of the deceased, heard a noise in the street and on going down found Tregeagle lying in the water table practically naked and unconscious. After wrapping Tregeagle in a rug Miners fetched Police Constable Davies. They found the doors of Tregeagle's house bolted and the bedroom window open. The door was forced and Tregeagle carried in. He did not regain consciousness and died on Wednesday afternoon, having been attended by Dr Bennetts. It was stated that there had been nothing unusual in the deceased's manner prior to his being found by Miners, but Harriet Roberts who took his tea to him on Monday afternoon said he was then looking bad. The deceased's daughter, who is deaf and nearly blind and was in the house when her father was found, was not called. The jury returned a verdict of 'Death from injuries received by a fall from a window'.

Royal Cornwall Gazette – 8th April 1909
Burning Fatality at Tregony

Mr E.L. Carlyon held an Inquest at Tregony on Thursday concerning the death of Amelia Georgina Elliott, 48 yrs, wife of Arthur Treffry Elliott, farmer. Miss M.J.R. Elliott said the deceased resided with them and on Thursday spent the day in her bedroom. The witness left her at 8.20 p.m. sitting on a chair by the fire and a little later found her badly burnt. Miss S.H. Elliott said that about 9.40 p.m. she smelt fire and went to the bedroom and found the deceased in a sitting position on the floor with her clothes smouldering. There was a candle on the dressing table and in her opinion the deceased's cape caught fire. The deceased was well able to look after herself but was not strong and had been under the doctor's care for some time. Dr Clover said he got to the house about 11.20 p.m. and found the deceased very severely burnt, nearly all of her clothes being burnt off. She was rather blind and clearly of poor intellect but required no special looking after and could go about with safety. He did not think the slightest blame rested on the Misses Elliot for leaving her alone. The jury returned a verdict of "accidentally burnt" and entirely exonerated the Misses Elliott from blame'.

Royal Cornwall Gazette – 16th September 1915
Four Children Die in Twelve Months – Cornelly Parents Censured.

'Mr E.L. Carlyon held an Inquest at Cornelly touching on the death at Cornelly on Monday of A.W. [identity withheld], aged 4 weeks, the son of J.W. [identity withheld] of Dabb's Hill Cottage, Cornelly. The Coroner said that the child was supposed to be sickly from birth, and the mother said she fed it on cow's milk for about two weeks. It became worse and would not take it and she tried malt milk but the child gradually got worse and died. It was for the jury to decide whether or not the woman properly looked after the child and did all she could to keep it alive. It was a peculiar fact that this was the fourth child of the family which had died *in the past twelve months. It might be natural but it was an extraordinary fact. The district nurse, Nurse Ash, was not satisfied that everything was done for the child and she suggested that Dr Bonar ought to see it, but when he called at the house on three occasions the woman refused to let him see the child. If the child was unable to take milk, the parents ought to have sought medical advice from a doctor.*

After hearing from witnesses and the parents, the jury returned a verdict that death was due to the want of sufficient food or improper feeding and exonerated Dr Bonar from blame. The parents deserved the severest censure in not calling medical attention. The Coroner addressing the parents said that the jury had taken a very lenient view as he thought that their actions were near the line to a criminal charge of manslaughter. The parents had been very callous but the jury thought it was due to ignorance rather than criminal intent'.

Reference

1   South Powder Petty Sessions Court Registers – County Record Office (AD81/25-27).

Chapter 12

THE GOOD OLD DAYS

The expression is often used without thinking, mostly by the elderly, but by some younger people too, who have not experienced them. We, who have lived in the latter part of the last century [1800s], like to remember all the good things and happy days of which there were many. Although wages were low, prices were too, everything being dirt-cheap and I doubt if there are many, especially the working class or businessmen, who would like to return to those good old days. It is recognised by all that a peaceful revolution has taken place in Britain during the last 50 years and for me to attempt to explain it all would be impossible, but to make a beginning, motor transport has played a major part in commerce and farming, followed by electricity, telephones, radio and piped water and sewerage schemes. The introduction of the Welfare State of today seems to me far better than the good old days of yesterday.

Tregony old folks of the early 1900s. Mr Edward Cox and his wife Ann, outside their home at Chapel Terrace. They both died in 1905. He was aged 91yrs and she was 95. Their granddaughter, Miss Mary Annie Woolcock is on the left.

With this in mind, I will describe the Village and how the people lived. First there was only one independent gentleman and he resided at Penlee, and apart from the Rector and the Doctor, the others would be businessmen and craftsmen and the rest; the majority would be labourers. Living conditions were determined as now, by wages and salaries. I can only speak of the wage earners. The wages of skilled craftsmen, such as masons, carpenters and blacksmiths, were about 18/- per week. The labourer's wage would be 15/- per week of six days from 7 a.m. to 5 p.m., most of them going to the farms and doing a little on Sundays as well, as horsemen or bullock men. They usually had some little 'perks' for this but at that time there were no guaranteed wages or hours.

I must now tell of home life and to begin with my own home. We were a family of nine with four boys and three girls. My father was a jobbing man with a pony and trap, dealing in potatoes, eggs and anything else, to make a living. He also did jobbing gardening and in the Winter he spent much time going from farm clipping horses, which was quite a big job with hundreds of horses about. Whilst on horses, in Tregony alone there would be about thirty, with twenty ponies and a large number of donkeys. These were the nights when no motor horns disturbed us, but I've been awakened many a night by the braying of the dear old donkeys calling each other.

Thinking back on the 'good old days', I can see that it was the mothers who performed the miracles of rearing a family, which averaged four children in those days, on 15/- per week. It must surely have been a problem, but the mothers overcame them and I think country children were then blessed according to the industrial areas. Food was number one, after which came clothes, which had to be governed by the pocket, and much of it had to be home-made and cut down, etc.

In the grocers, 'happeths' (½d worth) and 'penneths' (1d worth) was the com-

Lower Fore Street, Tregony, taken from a postcard dated 1912. A bread van owned by H. William's Steam Bakery of Probus delivers to the Village. A few yards away stands a policeman [possibly Sgt Kendall] weighing up the situation!

The pilchard cart, early 1900s. The location is not Tregony, but believed to be somewhere in the Roseland or Mevagissey areas. These sellers often travelled inland and sold fish directly from their carts.

mon purchase, goods were mostly sold by measure or weight, packed commodities were rare and an order for 4/- or 5/- was as much as one could carry. Children

A typical 'Sunday Best' suit for a young boy of the early 1900s

would be happy with a ha'penny or penny to spend on sweets – often they would ask the shopkeeper for a 'happeth' mixed from two bottles, yet the good lady would oblige. In the cottages, flour, potatoes, beef, pork and fish were the staple food. Flour and potatoes were mostly bought by the sack and never less than a peck, as practically all foods were home-baked in cloam or Town Ovens and the present fancies were unknown.

It was in the mid 1890s that the first baker's cart came to Tregony. Barm had been used up to that time, instead of yeast. (Barm, the froth skimming of brewing of beer). Each pub had their days of brewing and it

An example of 'Sunday Best' clothes for a young girl in the early 1900s.

146

was sold for ½d or 1d per jug. I have fetched it many a time.

Beef was very cheap, steak at 6d, other cuts at 4d per lb. and 2d or 3d of bits made a good dinner. A hock of beef would last for three meals, (this was boiling beef of course) and pork was 4d to 5d per lb. Pilchards were seven or eight a penny and often bought by the 100 for salting. Ours were salted in a large brown glazed earthenware

Joseph Greet [the photographer] with a relative 'scraping' a pig after it had been slaughtered for its meat.

pan. Butter too was salted when cheap in the summer months from the farms at 6d or 7d per lb. Salted butter was sold in the shops too; it came, I remember, in large wooden boxes. Turnips were three a penny, a large flatpoll cabbage 2d, with good scalded milk at ½d per quart. With these cheap foods, plus rabbit pies and a good rick of faggots in the garden, not many went hungry in the country.

Clothing and footwear, however, was not an easy matter, although prices were so low. Boots for boys cost 2/11d upward. Most boys had only one pair until they went to work. A boy could be fitted out for 10/-; consisting of a coat and trousers for 5/-, a cap 6d, collar 6d, boots and a bow or tie, and he was ready for Sunday School. Shirts were usually home-made and stockings knitted at home or by an old lady, who knitted mine for 4d per pair. I don't know much about girls' clothes, but prices were similar, so that altogether, mothers had to rack their brains.

There were dressmakers in Tregony at that time and one used to come to our house, with her two apprentices and bringing her machine for a day and charging 2/- or 3/-. They would do some conjuring with old clothes, remaking, etc. This was common to all and very necessary to keep out of debt and little if any was thrown in the rag bag.

The old people had two main wishes, one they would not have to ask for relief (how different from today) and the other hoping they would not be buried by the Parish. Too many were, as Parish Pay was only 2/6d to 3/- per week and for children 1/6d pence. The Relieving Officer came to a cottage one day a week and those who could had to collect their pay. If you wonder how those 'on the Parish' existed, to help they gathered wood from the hedges, the women did a bit of 'baby-sitting' for a neighbour or were invited out at times for a meal, besides doing a bit of darning or knitting when they could. The old men gathered sticks or found some job earning a 6d and if they had no relatives or friends when they were unable to help themselves, the Workhouse would be their last home before being brought back home to their resting place and that to me was a very sad and pathetic sight; the end of perhaps an old ploughman as a pauper.

SOCIAL WELFARE
(Additional information compiled by Franklin Grigg)

The period covered by this book pre-dates the arrival into the Village of such basic facilities as electricity, mains water and a public sewage system. Prior to this residents relied on wells or hand pumps for water, candles or paraffin lamps for lighting and 'dry' bucket privies for toilets. The living conditions in some of the Tregony houses were very dire, mainly because of poverty and the lack of public funds to improve public utilities. On the other hand, the more affluent tradesmen, farmers, professionals and independents were able to afford their own private utilities and also employed others to carry out the domestic work.

By the 1890s, the control of public health, medical care and public assistance was gradually being regulated in a more centralised and liberal fashion, as opposed to the older, Parish framework, but even so, public funds were limited, and standards very basic[1]. The feared

Local ladies gathering firewood, Tregony 1917. (L-r) Mrs Mary Toms, Miss Fanny Spear, Mrs Catherine Grose and Mrs Ada Barnicoat.

Union Workhouses were still in existence, catering for the destitute, who were either sick and/or homeless. Persons from Tregony were removed to the St Clement's Workhouse at Truro. Most of us remember the building by its later name, the Truro Isolation Hospital in Tregolls Road. Tregony individuals who were poor and had accommodation, were able to apply for the weekly 'Parish Pay', but they had to endure the degrading inquisitions of the Relieving Officer's home visits to check that the system was not being abused.

The Public Health Act, 1875 created Sanitary Districts and vested its Committees with powers to inspect and enforce aspects of public health. Tregony came within the Truro Rural District Council Area.

In 1889, the Cornwall County Council held their first meeting and gradually began to take powers to regulate and run many of the social and health facilities that we know today, but progress was slow.

For the treatment of injuries and illnesses, Tregonians in the 1890s, depended on the paid services of the local doctor, yet some could not afford him. A 'Parish' doctor would have been accessible to the really poor. The Royal Cornwall Infirmary at Truro which had been in existence since the 1790s was on a much smaller scale than today. A trip to Truro in a horse and waggon or carriage would have been a harrowing experience for the sick or seriously injured. The majority of the working-class men of Tregony were members of the St James's Order of the Oddfellows, (Friendly Society), thus affording them and their families, reasonable funds to seek medical attention from the town doctor. Indispensable was the local 'wise' old lady who had the 'knowledge' to deliver babies, layout the dead, give herbal remedies and charm away warts. Many country folk trusted these rural sages for advice and remedies.

By the early 1900s, Tregony and Ruan Parishes had formed a Nursing Association which raised funds to pay to secure a trained nurse to visit and attend the sick and injured of the area.

Relevant Newspaper Articles of the Day

Royal Cornwall Gazette – 22nd December 1892
Insanitation at Tregony

'Dr Bonar reported as Medical Officer of the Truro Union (Eastern District), that the district was entirely free from any infectious diseases. A house-to-house inspection had been carried out in the remaining part of Tregony which revealed a very unsatisfactory state of affairs. At Gurney Row, formed of two blocks of old, dirty, dilapidated houses, found pigs, fowls, & etc, kept in little ill-ventilated cribs close to the back doors of the cottages. In one instance the urine of the pigs had made a pool immediately in front of the door. Scavenging and cleaning

of the privies, which did exist, were not attempted; one built by the landlord for the conven-
ience of his tenant had not been cleaned out, so several people told him, for three years. It
was a case of laziness and filth and the sanitary Inspector ought to lose no time in exercising
his authority in the matter'.

Royal Cornwall Gazette – 7th April 1898
St John's Ambulance Lectures

'A course of lectures on 'Ambulance Work or First Aid to the Injured' was given by Dr Bonar
at Probus and Tregoney during the month of February. At each place they were well attend-
ed, the lectures being given admirably. The meetings were open to all, and any person could
have sat for examination; but no civilians rose to the occasion. Five local members of the
Cornwall Constabulary who attended the lectures were the only persons who were examined
and they all passed with the highest honours'.

Royal Cornwall Gazette – 5th May 1898
Village Sanitation in the Truro Union

(A summary of the recommendations given in a report by Dr Bonar to the Sanitary
Committee of the Truro Rural District Council)

That all private wells be securely protected from surface drainage; that the contents of
privies, ash-pits, cess-pools, etc, should, immediately on removal be taken to a distance of at
least 80 feet from the well or dug into the earth at the most remote part of the garden; and
that unregistered dairies come under the same control as registered ones. The Doctor added
that he had seen milk to be sold in Truro stored in local rooms, the condition of which was
such, that had the consumers seen it, they would not have drunk the milk.

Royal Cornwall Gazette – 23rd April 1908
Cornish Midwives.

'The Midwives Committee of Cornwall County Council met on Thursday. Dr Sharp of Truro
wrote that there was not the slightest improvement in the method of practice by midwives.
None of the uncertified midwives had any knowledge of the use of a thermometer, nor did they
use any disinfecting lotion for their hands. The Committee approved a scheme for further
training'.

Royal Cornwall Gazette – 19th March 1914
Truro R.D.C Meeting - Houses at Tregoney

'During a discussion on bad houses at Tregony, it was stated that the walls of a house belong-
ing to Miss Dunstan were hanging three feet over the road and it was very dangerous. Mr

Thompson stated, "I admit it, but there are other walls in Tregoney equally as bad". (laughter)

Royal Cornwall Gazette - 6th November 1918
Tregoney – The Flu

'The dreaded disease has made its presence felt keenly and almost every house has been visited. In some cases the whole family has been laid down at the same time. Some cases are of a serious character and both bus proprietors are laid up with pneumonia. On Sunday morning last the Rev F.W. King was taken ill just as the service commenced at the Parish Church, and had to be taken home'.

Royal Cornwall Gazette – 13th November 1918
Influenza Victim

'The flu is still raging and claimed another victim during the last week in the three-year-old child (Sabina Pearl)

St Cuby's Well in the 1920s. A pump had been fitted. Unknown source

of Gunner John and Mrs Towsey. The child was ill only a few days and died of pneumonia. The funeral took place on Sunday and was largely attended. Much sympathy is felt with the parents, especially as Mrs Towsey was seriously ill with the same disease at the time of the child's death'.

Royal Cornwall Gazette – 27th November 1918
Destructive Rodents – Tregony

'In addition to the damage to the corn crops by heavy rain, we now learn that great injury is being done to the stacks of corn in the locality by rats. It is reported that on one farm alone over 200 of these destructive rodents were destroyed in a week'.

Giggen Well and Pump, July 1989. The area was renovated and a replica pump installed by the following local gents: (l-r) Leo Lidgey, George Barnicoat, Dalby Michell and Martin Berryman. Source Mr William Barnicoat

Giggen Pump in 1992. The Author

Royal Cornwall Gazette – 16th July 1903
Fatal Accident at Tregony. Claim Under the Workmen's Compensation Act (Summary)

His Honour Judge Granger had before him at Truro County Court on Saturday an application by Joseph Tonkin, Tregoney, for an award of £163. 16s. under the Act, against Messrs Thompson Bros., seed merchants & farmers, Tregoney. The son of the applicant, while engaged in straw pressing for the respondents, met with an accident by which his foot was crushed. The limb was amputated, but gangrene set in and the leg was cut off, but eventually death took place. After legal arguments Mr Tonkin was awarded £67, in addition to the £50 paid into the court, with costs.

Royal Cornwall Gazette – 28th November 1901
Advert – Old False Teeth Bought

'Many people have old or disused false teeth. Send your teeth to R.D. & J.B. Fraser Ltd., Princess Street, Ipswich, (established 1833) and they will remit the utmost value by return, or make you best offer. Largest and oldest buyers of old false teeth in the world'.

Royal Cornwall Gazette – 26th November 1919
Resident's Mishap

'Whilst Mr Joseph Barnicoat, carpenter of Tregoney, was pulling a bundle of straw out of a rick, the cord of the bundle broke and he fell backwards, breaking his ankle. The accident happened at Barn Farm and he had to crawl out to the highway some distance off, when a passing cart conveyed the sufferer to his home where he was attended by Dr. Ashby'.

26 March 1912, the official opening of the pump in The Square by Miss Harvey Williams, formerly of Penlee. The sinking of a well and erection of the pump was funded by public subscription to commemorate the Coronation of George V.

Public Wells/Pumps in Tregony

Mains electricity, water and sewage came to the Village in stages between the 1930s and the 1950s but, initially, only a few houses were joined to the systems, as many of the householders could not afford the connection charges. The majority of the population had to rely on water supplied from public wells or hand pumps. These were strategically placed throughout the Village, but for some it meant a 'long carry' with 'pails' (buckets) or pitchers of water. Here are details of the main water sources:

St Cuby's Well. *This ancient well, located off Cuby Lane (just past the Police Station), provided water to the top end of Tregony. It was more of a hole in the base of a hedge filled by spring water, than a deep well. In the early 1900s a wooden door was fitted and a hand pump provided. Although now surrounded by undergrowth, it is still possible to find the well.*

Stanbury Row Well. *The well was sited at the far end of the Row. It was about three to four feet deep and even in times of drought, it was able to supply the Village with sufficient water, even when other wells were dry. The well is no longer visible as it has been filled in and covered. [There was also a second private well which was located on the right hand side several yards along the Row.]*

An early 1920s postcard looking down towards The Square. The walls surrounding the pump can clearly be seen to the right of the War Memorial. Rexatone Series

The restored Coronation Memorial Stone. Originally it was built into the wall surrounding the pump in the Village Square. The Author 1997

Giggen Well & Pump. This was another ancient water source which was situated at the bottom of the hill, just below the Village Hall. Originally it would have provided water to the small community that resided nearby. In 1989, a small group of local enthusiasts renovated the area, and sited a new replica pump and a wooden seat. A contemporary, ornate, granite column was positioned on the adjoining small grass area, in the year 2000, by the company which had developed the nearby new estate of houses named 'The Park'.

It is known that a subterranean stream runs from Fore Street, under the Village Hall and down to where the pump is located. This spring at one time must have been on the surface, as a 1787 map showed 'Drunken Bridge' sited in Fore Street, roughly where the old Methodist Sunday School building is today. This bridge would have spanned the stream.

The Square. The costs of sinking this twenty-five feet well and the erecting of a hand pump were met by public subscription. It was inaugurated to commemorate the Coronation of King George V in 1911. An inscribed granite stone was affixed to the wall which surrounded the pump. However, by the 1960s, the pump had been removed and in 1996, the late Mr Ken

The covered well in Well Street, early 1900s. The name of the lady is unknown.

154

Dowrick and the Author found the long-discarded, memorial stone lying nearby, unrecognised and damaged. A year later, the Parish Council had the stone repaired and reset. In 2001, the family of the late Mr Fernley Blackler re-installed a pump in his memory.

Well Street. *Once a covered well, this was located directly outside the top doorway of number 5, Well Street [The old Town Oven]. It had steps leading down to the water level. The brick canopy structure was dismantled in the 1950s. A metal manhole cover still marks the spot. Although it appeared to have been used by the public for many years, there was a great debate in 1920 concerning ownership. (See chapter 10).*

Daddiport Well & Pump. *[Also known as 'Bottom Town Pump']*
This well supplied water for the people at the lower end of Tregony Hill. The pump has now been removed and the well filled in. It was located at the base of Reskivers Hill, on the site of a newly constructed house, named 'Quay House'. Originally access was gained to the pump via a footpath which ran beside the old 'blacksmith shop' at the bottom of Tregony Hill.

Well Street, Tregony 1992. The brick housing over the well has been removed and the entrance is now secured with a metal cover. The Author

Reference

1   'The Jubilee of County Councils' (Cornwall edition) - Book published by Evans Brothers Ltd, London 1939.

Chapter 13

THE ADJOINING DISTRICT

(An additional chapter compiled by Franklin Grigg)

In ecclesiastical terms, the Parishes of Tregony St James (the old Village Parish) and the adjoining Cuby, Cornelly and Veryan were originally all separate. As time has progressed, events and geographical features have tended to draw the Parishes into a closer unit, which is based on Tregony. The following are examples of this association:

By 1549 the Parish Church of Tregony St James had been abandoned because of flooding and the congregation moved to nearby Cuby Parish Church. Thus St Cuby's became the Mother Church of both Tregony and Cuby.

Cornelly is still an independent Parish but in 1973 it became part of the United Benefice of Tregony with St Cuby and it has since been administered by the Rector of Tregony. Prior to 1973 the church came under the care of the Parish of Probus.

Veryan is a completely independent Parish. The Church is situated approximately five miles from Tregony. For record purposes, however, Veryan has been closely associated with Tregony as the Northern part of Veryan's Parish boundary extends close to the bottom of

Tregony Hill. The division follows the small stream which flows under Daddiport Bridge and continues down the Fal River as far as Porters in Ruan Road.

Cuby Parish

The country area to the north and east of the Tregony Village is a part of the ancient Parish of Cuby. As previously mentioned, the Mother Church of St Cuby is shared with the Township of Tregony. Also notable, is the fact that the location of St Cuby's Church and the south-western edge of Cuby Parish boundary encroaches onto the top of Tregony, i.e. it runs along Back Lane, between the Parish Church and the Church Hall.

Cuby House, Tregony, circa 1900.

Pitts Down Farm, Cuby, approx. 1909. The Grigg family pose with workmen around the hayrick. (Front, l-r) Colan Grigg, uncle; u/k youth; Edith Grigg; Albert J. Grigg, Olive Grigg; May Grigg; Harold Grigg, on horse; Eldred H. Grigg, father of children. Of the workmen, only Dick Cloke can be identified, 2nd from left.

Great Gargus Farmhouse, Cuby, circa 1905. The Julyan family had rebuilt the house only a few years previously.

157

Members of the Julyan family outside Great Gargus Farmhouse in about 1905.

The bottom of Dabb's Hill, Cornelly, early 1900s. A lady can be seen standing in the doorway of Dabb's Hill Cottage. Washing is drying on the bushes in the garden and three children are sitting on the bank beside the road.

According to the 1902 Kelly's Directory, Cuby Parish covered an area of some 2,262 acres with a population of 117. Apart from Cuby House [the large residence opposite the Parish Church] and a very few isolated cottages, the remaining dwellings within the Parish were farms. The principal landowners were Viscount Falmouth of Tregothnan and John Charles William of Caerhays Castle.

Listed in 1902 were:
    Rosevallen – Thos Wm. Elliott, farmer.
    Newton – Ralph Freethy, farmer.
    Pittsdown – Eldrerd Harold Grigg, farmer.
    Little Gargus – John Hawkins, farmer.
    Goviley Major – Thomas Andrew Holman, farmer.
    Great Gargus - Richard Julyan, farmer.
    Holboat – John Thomas Knight, farmer.
    Treluckey – George Parsons, farm bailiff to Wm. Tremain of Treluckey.
    Great Holboat – James Rogers, farmer.
    Pencose – Ernest Thomas, farmer.
    Tregonhayne – Peter & Giles Wm. Thomson, farmers.
    Carveth – P & G.T. Thomson, farmers and manure agents.
    Goviley Vean – Mrs Sarah Treffry, farmer.

These farms employed many of the Tregony 'slingers', mentioned by Mr Frank Greet.

Freewater Lodge, circa 1910 [which is actually in Probus Parish]. Beaters from Trewarthenick Estate taking a breather from the estate shoot. In the background, Miss Ethel Lyndon is standing in the doorway of the Lodge.

The Dawe family outside of Mellingoose Farm House, Cornelly in about 1916. The house has since been demolished. (L-r) Lewis Dawe with his dog; Ella Payne & Olga Dawe [in the cart]; John [Jack] Dawe; Marge Payne and Reg Dawe. [Under the white blob were concealed Maggie and Nan Dawe. These two older ladies were displeased with their appearances and obliterated themselves from the negative].

Cornelly Parish Church in the early 1900s. Note the leaning bell tower. The identities of the three people are unknown.

Cornelly Parish

This rural and sparsely populated Parish is situated to the east of Tregony. The River Fal forms a natural boundary between both Parishes.

Cornelly Church

The Parish has an ancient, little Parish Church with a slight, leaning tower. Seemingly, the name 'Cornelly' is derived from the name of St Cornelly or in Latin, Cornelius[1] A Pope and Martyr, he was also the Patron Saint of Horned Animals. The Church which stands on a raised site overlooking the River Fal may have been an ancient Iron Age Round.

Trewarthenick House

The chief landowner and Lord of the Manor of Cornelly resided in the large mansion named Trewarthenick. In 1640 the house and the 'Manor' properties were purchased by the Gregor Family, who in time renovated and improved both the Church and the mansion. The succession passed from daughters and cousins to Sir Lewis Molesworth in 1896, and Mr Paul Arundel Welman in 1913. The Welmans left the big house in 1958. It is now converted into private flats.

Trewarthenick House, Cornelly in the early 1900s or possibly before. Workmen excavating earth for the restructuring of the gardens. In the 1930s, the wing on the left-hand side was demolished after a serious fire had damaged the structure.

Trewarthenick House, circa 1910. Another view. The workman is thought to be Bob Lyndon.

Trewarthenick House, about 1910. A gathering or fete in the grounds of the house.

The Gregor Arms

Owned by the Trewarthenick Estate, and aptly named, 'Gregor Arms', the Parish once boasted its own Public House. It was located at the foot of Dabb's Hill in the large building that is now known as Gregor House. It closed its doors in June of 1918 when it was rented out as a private dwelling-house. For a while, part of the premises was used by a co-operative as a cheese-making factory.

Royal Cornwall Gazette – 21st August 1918 – Cheese Making

'The local Co-operative Cheese Society, whose factory is at the old Gregor Arms, is having a successful season. Over 100 gallons of milk are dealt with daily. It has not yet been decided whether the Society will continue after the period for which the County Council plant and instructress were loaned, but it is believed that if the co-operative was extended to other articles besides cheese connected with the farming industry, it would not only prove profitable to its members, but be of much assistance to the district'.

The 1902 Kelly's Directory gave the land area of the Parish as 1361 acres and the population numbered 71 persons.

The Gregor Arms Public House, Cornelly, circa 1910. Mr and Mrs Glanville, the licensees are standing in the doorway. The gent with the pony and trap is Mr John A. Nicholls of Tredinnick Farm, Veryan. A steam lorry from T. Rowse & Sons, Geen Mill, Probus is delivering grain for beer making.

Looking back at Tregony Bridge from Cornelly. On the back of this photo of about 1898 was writ-ten, 'a stopping off point on the way to Truro market'. This obviously referred to the nearby Gregor Arms.

The principal inhabitants were

> *Trewarthenick House – Sir Lewis William Molesworth, M.P., D.L., J.P.*
>
> *Killiow – Samuel Bennett, farmer.*
>
> *Grogarth Wallace – Alfred Bennett, farmer.*
>
> *Penpell – Thomas Bennetto, farmer.*
>
> *Gregor Arms Public House – William Evans.*
>
> *Gamekeeper to Sir L.W. Molesworth – Henry Finch.*
>
> *Land Steward to Sir L.W. Molesworth – James Hoare.*
>
> *Head Gardener at Trewarthenick House – William McCreath.*
>
> *Great Grogarth – Jn. P. Nicholls, farmer.*

Cornelly, Additional Information

Newspaper Items

Royal Cornwall Gazette – 6th June 1912
The Late Sir Lewis Molesworth – Funeral at Cornelly (Summary)

'Sir Lewis Wm. Molesworth, eleventh Baronet of Trewarthenick, who died suddenly on Wednesday week at Torquay, was formerly Unionist Member of Parliament for South East

Cornwall. The remains were brought to Trewarthenick on Friday and the coffin was laid in his study on a plain table with a purple pall, surrounded by flowers. In accordance with his expressed wishes, and hatred of trappings of death, the funeral arrangements were of the simplest nature. The coffin was carried both from the railway station and to the little churchyard at Cornelly on his own four-wheeled buggy. By the wishes of Lady Molesworth, no family wreaths were sent but each plucked a bunch of bloom in the garden and placed them on the coffin, and these with the wreath from the tenants were the only floral tributes placed thereon. The grave was lined with moss and ferns and white flowers by the head gardener'.

Royal Cornwall Gazette – 2nd October 1912
Death of Lady Molesworth (Summary)

'We record with regret the death of Lady Jane Graham Molesworth, widow of Sir Lewis Molesworth, which took place on Thursday evening at Trewarthenick, at the age of 53 years. Her ladyship was sitting near an open widow when a wasp alighted on her neck and stung her. She hurried upstairs and applied ammonia and on returning to the room complained of palpitations and collapsed, dying within twenty minutes.

Mr E. Carlyon (Coroner) held an Inquest at the house on Friday morning. After hearing from witnesses the jury (Rev Philip E. Brown, Vicar of Tregoney, being the Foreman) returned a verdict of "Death from syncope, caused by the sting of a wasp".

Lady Molesworth was the second daughter of Brigadier General Daniel Marsh Frost of St

Cornelly Parish Church on the 1st June 1912 – the funeral of Sir Lewis William Molesworth, age 58 years of Trewarthenick, Cornelly.

13th Oct 1921 – The official opening of the Trewarthenick, former private driveway, as a public road. Mr Hawk, Chairman of Cornwall County Council, performed the ceremony. CRO-(AD545/2)

Louis, North America. She was extremely popular and had been a very beautiful woman. After the death of her husband, Lady Molesworth sold her house in Great Cumberland Place, where in former days she entertained a good deal during the London season.

The Opening of the New Road at Trewarthenick.

Accounts of road traffic accidents reveal how dangerous the public road was for vehicles travelling between Truro and Tregony. Traffic had to negotiate the steep gradients of Freewater Hill and Dabb's Hill. The birth of the County Council promoted negotiations and plans for a new road to run from Freewater Lodge via the Trewarthenick private drive on to the Gregor Arms; thus offering a safer alternative route.

Royal Cornwall Gazette – 28th January 1920
Truro Rural District Council – The New Tregoney Road

'Mr Samuels, Road Board Engineer, said the County Council had now come to an agreement with Capt. Welman of Trewarthenick as to the sum to be paid for taking over the drive for use of the public. The C.C. now proposed to carry through the scheme from Freewater Hill to Trewarthenick Drive, following the drive round and through the district road from Trewarthenick to the Gregor Arms.

Royal Cornwall Gazette – 19th October 1921 (summary)
Greatly Improved Route to Tregoney - Trewarthenick Ceremony

'Amongst relief work schemes which have been undertaken in Cornwall, none is of a more useful nature than the new Trewarthenick road by which it is now possible to enter Tregoney without encountering the very steep and dangerous hills known as Freewater and Dabb's Hill. The official opening ceremony took place on the 13th October 1921 by Mr Hawk, the Chairman of the Cornwall County Council. The widening and improvement of the private drive into a public road commenced in June 1920 and had been carried out by direct labour (including married ex-servicemen engaged through the Labour Exchange). The estimated cost of the work was £10,300 and the length of the road under construction being 1,850 yards.

Royal Cornwall Gazette – 3st August 1921
Steward Shot At From Roadside

'Mr W.A. Johns, steward of the Trewarthenick Estate, had an alarming experience last evening. He was driving through Killiow Lane from Grampound Road Station to Trewarthenick at 8.45 p.m. when suddenly a man came out of the plantation and shouted, "Stop." Mr Johns drove on rapidly whereupon the man fired at him with a revolver, the bullet (it was found later) passing through the bottom of the door of the jingle and striking the step-iron. Mr Johns was unable to identify the man, but described him as being short, very stout, of dark complexion and between 30 and 40 years of age. He was wearing a check coat'. [Whether the alleged crime was ever solved is unknown.]

The Keast Family of Hay Barton, near Reskivers, Veryan, circa 1893. They are still in mourning for Mr Stephen Keast [husband & father]. (L-r) Lillian; Edith; Mrs Lavinia Keast; Mabel; Ellen [Nellie]; and Ethel.

Veryan Parish

Veryan is by far the biggest of the Parishes adjoining Tregony. The 1902 Kelly's Directory gave the acreage of the Parish as 5,751 and the population as 1,059.

The small communities at Reskivers, Bessy Beneath, Daddiport and Ruan Road, although situated within the Parish of Veryan, were much closer to Tregony and the people used the facilities in the Village for most of their necessities, e.g. schooling, shopping, medical, etc. One exception was their spiritual needs. Many of the families preferred to travel a greater distance to their 'home' Parish Church at Veryan for baptisms, marriages and funerals.

Taken from the 1902 Kelly's Directory, here is a list of homesteads and persons within distance of Tregony:

Daddiport - Mrs Eliza Baker.

Bessy Beneath – Thomas Barnicoat, blacksmith.

Mount Folley – James Broad, farmer.

Castlends – William Chapman, farmer.

Lower Trencreek – John Dustow, farmer.

Hay – Stephen Keast.

Reskivers – John Kemp, farmer.

Tredennick – Jn. Arthur Nicholls, farmer.

Hay Barton, approx. 1913, another photo of the Keast Family. (L-r) Lilly; Ethel; Mrs Lavinia Keast; and Ellen [Nellie]. In the background is Mr Eames Hawkey, the farm manager.

Early 1900s renovations to Hay Cottages [accommodation for the labourers at Hay Barton]. The old cob walls are being redressed with brick.

A modern photo of the old Hay Cottages. They have now been converted into a single house which is popularly known as 'The owl and Pussycat' because of the statues of these creatures located on the chimney tops. The Author 1997

Reference

1   Cornelly Parish Church History booklet 1973 – copy with the Author.

Chapter 14

THE FIRST WORLD WAR 1914-1918

(An additional chapter compiled by Franklin Grigg)

- *War was declared on the 4th August 1914.*
- *The War against the Turks ended with their capitulation on the 30th October 1918.*
- *The conflict against Germany ended with their surrender and the Armistice came into effect at 11 a.m. on 11th November 1918.*
- *However, other hostilities continued, namely, the Allied intervention in the Russian Civil War on the side of the White Russians. The British involvement ended in October 1919. Further flash-points were in the North West Frontier of India and also Persia.*

*A*ll communities, and Tregony was no exception, suffered the great life-changing physical and social repercussions which the First World War had impacted on the population. Not only the fighting forces but everyone was to experience revised social attitudes and working practices. The greatest loss and suffering, of course, was by the families of the vast number of men and women who did not survive the conflict and those who had received such horrible wounds as to render them incapacitated.

The following is a simple, patriotic poem which best speaks the local sentiment of those times. It was printed in the Royal Cornwall Gazette on the 16th April 1919. The author's name is unknown.

THE TREGONEY VOLUNTEERS

"In the days of voluntary recruiting the ancient Borough had by far the highest average for the county and, unfortunately, has the highest for those making the supreme sacrifice in the War. A correspondent sends the following verses in honour of the deeds of her sons":

"When the storms of war burst upon us,
Old Tregoney responded to the call,
And headed the list for the County
With her volunteers – one and all.

From lads who were little more than kiddies,
To men who were well advanced in years,
They marched out to fight for King and Country.
And we're proud of our Tregoney volunteers.

Chorus
Three cheers for the Tregoney volunteers,
Three cheers for our brave volunteers,
Who marched out to fight for King and Country,
Three cheers for the Tregoney volunteers.

Now that the Great War is over,
Our lads will return from the front;
On the mine-strewn sea and the trenches
They've been bearing the grim battle brunt.
Not a word of complaint have they uttered,
To them death really had no fears;
They have all done their bit for King and Country,
And we're proud of our Tregoney volunteers.

Many of our brave lads have fallen
Far away from those they love so dear;
Their memories will ever live amongst us,
Though their voices we never more shall hear.
They would tell us not to grieve about them,
And bid us wipe away the tears,
For they died proudly at their post of duty,
And we're proud of our Tregoney volunteers."

War Memorials

Tregony has two public War Memorials. The main one, which is situated in The Village Square, consists of a large granite obelisk inscribing the names of the men from the district who (1) fought in the War and (2) died therein. (For fuller details of the men who are recorded, see Appendices A and B at the back of this book. Also included is a casualty list from the

The War Memorial in the Village Square at Tregony, 1950. George Ellis Collection, Cornwall Centre

Second World War – Appendix C).

Another smaller memorial plaque is situated inside the Parish Church. It commemorates the names of those who died. [This roll-call differs slightly from the main Memorial].

*The following are the names of those listed on the **Memorial in Tregony Square** who did not survive the First World War:*

BEARD W.J.

BUCKINGHAM R.J.J.

BURLEY A.

CARHART R.T.

COLEMAN J.E. *(the correct initials were J.C.)*

CUTLER F.

GREET C.

HENWOOD H.

LEAN R.

LYNDON E.P.

LYNDON H.

MOUNTSTEPHEN W.N.

SPEAR C.J.

SPEAR J.H.

VINCENT J.H.

WARNE J.P.

*This following list contains the names of the persons killed who are remembered on the **Plaque in the Parish Church**:*

"*In loving memory of all from this Parish and District who died for freedom in the Great War, 1914-1919. Their hope is full of immortality. Erected by the parishioners and friends.*"

BARNICOAT Edwin

BARNICOAT Thomas

BEARD John

THE FOLLOWING HAVE MADE THE
SUPREME SACRIFICE FOR THEIR
KING & COUNTRY 1914-1918.
W. J. BEARD.
R. J. J. BUCKINGHAM.
A. BURLEY.
R. T. CARHART.
J. E. COLEMAN.
F. CUTLER.
C. GREET.
H. HENWOOD.
R. LEAN.
E. P. LYNDON.
H. LYNDON.
W. N. MOUNTSTEPHEN.
C. J. SPEAR.
J. H. SPEAR.
J. H. VINCENT.
J. P. WARNE.
GREATER LOVE HATH NO MAN
THAN THIS. THAT A MAN LAY DOWN
HIS LIFE FOR HIS FRIENDS.

The men who died. The Tregony War Memorial in The Square. The Author 1997

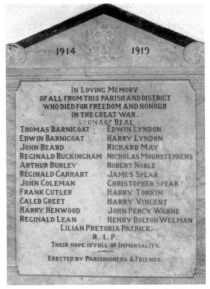

1914 · 1919

IN LOVING MEMORY
OF ALL FROM THIS PARISH AND DISTRICT
WHO DIED FOR FREEDOM AND HONOUR
IN THE GREAT WAR.

THOMAS BARNICOAT	EDWIN LYNDON
EDWIN BARNICOAT	HARRY LYNDON
JOHN BEARD	RICHARD MAY
REGINALD BUCKINGHAM	NICHOLAS MOUNSTEPHENS
ARTHUR BURLEY	ROBERT NOBLE
REGINALD CARHART	JAMES SPEAR
JOHN COLEMAN	CHRISTOPHER SPEAR
FRANK CUTLER	HARRY TONKIN
CALEB GREET	HARRY VINCENT
HARRY HENWOOD	JOHN PERCY WARNE
REGINALD LEAN	HENRY BOLTON WELMAN

LILIAN PRETORIA PATRICK.
R. I. P.
THEIR HOPE IS FULL OF IMMORTALITY.
ERECTED BY PARISHIONERS & FRIENDS.

The Tregony Parish Church Memorial to the fallen. The Author 2004

BUCKINGHAM *Reginald*
BURLEY *Arthur*
CARHART *Reginald*
COLEMAN *John*
CUTLER *Frank*
GREET *Caleb*
HENWOOD *Harry*
LEAN *Reginald*
LYNDON *Edwin*
LYNDON *Harry*
MAY *Richard*
MOUNTSTEPHEN *Nicholas*
NOBLE *Robert*
PATRICK *Lilian Pretoria*
REAL *Leonard*
SPEAR *Christopher*
SPEAR *James*
TONKIN *Harry*
VINCENT *Harry*
WARNE *John Percy*
WELMAN *Henry Bolton*

Private Lewis Burley [right] and Private Ford,
both of the Devon Regiment. Lewis survived
the war, the fate of the other is unknown.
Unknown source

The Home Front

A random selection from local newspaper articles of the time, reflect Tregony's participation.
Such items as news from the front, home preparations for the conflict and giving support to
the 'boys', were typical.

Royal Cornwall Gazette – 10th September 1914

'Richard Beard, Charles and Stephen Ford, Joseph Spear and Harry Linden have joined
Kitchener's Army and Sergt Leath, who has a son at the front, has volunteered for active serv-
ice. Mrs Welman, Trewarthenick, has organised a working party of ladies for the Red Cross
Society. A collection in the village for money to purchase materials realised £6'.

Royal Cornwall Gazette – 26th November 1914
Tregoney Parish Council

'On Monday the Council considered the circular dealing with "Distress Occasioned By War".
Mr E.W. Tonkin said that there was an ample supply of suitable land near the village for allot-

ments and many men in the place would be only glad to avail themselves of the opportunity of acquiring garden plots with a free supply of seeds, etc. Mr Lidgey said, "Many people would be glad to have land if they could have it free of charge". It was decided to hold a Parish Meeting'.

Royal Cornwall Gazette – 7th January 1915

'A social gathering, organised by Mr M. Barnicoat, was held yesterday evening week in aid of the Belgian Relief Fund. The company included two wounded Belgian officers who are staying at Trewarthenick. Songs were rendered by Mrs King, Misses Gladys Leath and Mabel Beard, Rev F.W. King, Messrs M. Barnicoat, Archie Barnicoat and S. Stephens and recitations by Mr Peter Thomson. The Belgian officers sang Belgian songs and the Belgian and French National Anthems. The proceeds amounted to £4'.

Royal Cornwall Gazette – 23rd November 1916 – Tregoney (summary)

'It is with very great regret that we have to report the deaths of two more of our gallant soldiers – Lieut Henry Bolton Welman R.M., third son of Mr and Mrs H. Welman of Trewarthenick; and of Private Harry Linden, second son of Mr Robert Linden. This district has now nine names on the Roll of Honour: Lieuts Welman and Cutler; Privates Mountstephen; J. Spear and Linden killed in action; Private C. Greet, drowned in the Royal Edward; W. Fugler, R.N.R., drowned in H.M.S. Formidable; and Private Chubb, A.S.C. who died in hospital. Private Alfred Peters, a native of Tregoney, who came all the way from New Zealand to fight for his country at the Dardanelles, was killed in France'.

Royal Cornwall Gazette – 4th January 1917 – Tregoney

'Efforts are being made to raise a fund for the purpose of sending each man from the Tregoney district serving in H.M. Forces, a New Year gift as a reminder of the fact that the service he is rendering to his country is not overlooked by those left at home. This district had by far the best results in the County in the days of voluntary recruiting. A social and dance realised upwards of £12, included in which was a sum raised by a raffle of a small pig, presented by Mr M. Barnicoat'.

Tregony 1917, Carrie Carbis, aged 14 yrs, collecting eggs to send to the troops.

Fresh Eggs for Our Boys

In 1991, Mrs Carrie Rickard neé Carbis of Tregony (since deceased) recalled that in 1917 when she was 14 years old, a scheme was set up to send fresh eggs to the troops at the front. The whole village participated. In particular, she remembered that with her friend Winnie Lidgey, she visited many of the local farms and collected eggs. As a personal touch, both of them endorsed the eggs with their names and addresses. Much excitement was felt when letters of thanks were received from these unknown troops. She often wondered what became of the men.

Arthur E. Nicholls in the uniform of the Royal Engineers. He was a professional soldier and was later promoted to Regimental Sgt. Major. He returned from the war. Unknown source

Royal Cornwall Gazette – 8th March 1917
Tregony and the Food Supply

'*A well attended public meeting to consider the question of increasing the food supply was held in the Council School on Friday evening. Mr Channon, Chairman of the Parish Council, presided, and stated that Lord Falmouth and Mr J.C. Williams, owners of land near the Village, would assist as far as possible in the matter of the land required. Some present thought it was rather late to start the scheme, but it was pointed out that the notices from the County Committee were not received in time.*

Mr Warne, Tregonhayne, offered a field but it was thought to be too far from the Village.

Mr G. Lidgey considered if they could not get land by compulsory powers nearby, it would be useless. The Chairman thought they had better approach the matter in a friendly spirit.

Mr E.W. Tonkin suggested that a committee be appointed to receive applications and then to arrange for the necessary land and supply of seed.

Mr A.J. Lovell moved an amendment that those requiring the allotments make their own arrangements. Mr G. Lidgey seconded and at this stage most of those present left the meeting.

The few that were left felt that some attempts should be made to increase the potato supply, as a shortage would

Gunner Solomon Mountstephens of the Royal Garrison Artillery. Although wounded, he did return home. Unknown source

Private Aaron Barnicoat of the Devon Regiment [The Author's Grandfather]. He survived the war. Source unknown

seriously affect large families. Suggestions were made but it was felt that any decisions then arrived at would not be authoritative'.

Royal Cornwall Gazette – 12th April 1917 – Tregoney

'In a letter home to his parents at the School House, Tregoney, Private Leonard Real, on behalf of the Tregoney boys, wished to thank the friends for their kindness in sending the New Year gifts out of the proceeds of the social held on Dec 23rd. The parcels were sent to Aden but were forwarded to them as they are now with the Egyptian Expeditionary Force'.

Royal Cornwall Gazette – 3rd May 1917 – In Memoriam

'SPEAR – In loving memory of Jim, the beloved son of Caroline and the late John Spear, of Stanbury Row, Tregoney, who was killed in action in France on May 5th, 1915. Sadly missed by his sorrowing mother, sisters and brothers'.

"God only knows who next may fall
Beneath death's chastening rod,
One must be first, but let us all
Prepare to meet our God".

Pte A. Barnicoat's Campaign Victory Medal. The Author 2004

Royal Cornwall Gazette – 10th May 1917 Tregoney Man's Miraculous Escape

'Mr Alwyn May, eldest son of Mr Richard May of Coronation Terrace, Tregoney, who has been in the Navy as an officer's steward for about five years, had a thrilling experience and a miraculous escape off the French coast on the 2nd inst. He was in one of H.M. destroyers engaged on escort duty which was struck by a mine in the early morning. The vessel was cut completely in two and the fore part disappeared with all on it almost instantly. Mr May was asleep in his bunk at the time of the explosion and rushed on deck with nothing on but a *flannel shirt. Hastily putting on a lifebelt he found himself in the water with seven survivors, when in a few minutes the after part of the destroyer sank. They were shortly afterwards picked up by a torpedo boat. About 16 of those on board were saved but 82 others perished. Mr May arrived home on Saturday for a few days leave'.*

Royal Cornwall Gazette – 4th October 1917 – Tregoney

'A large aeroplane, flying very low, passed over the village on Monday afternoon and caused much excitement'.

Royal Cornwall Gazette – 25th October 1917
'Our Day' in Cornwall

[This was a public appeal day on behalf of the sick and wounded sailors and soldiers]
'Our Day for the Tregoney united district was held on Saturday and the results were very gratifying, over £50 being realised. Flags were sold by Misses Chenoweth, Greet, C.&F. May, Blight and Patrick. There was a public tea followed by a jumble sale and a series of concerts in the Council schoolroom. The concerts were well attended. A regrettable incident occurred during the second concert. Mr A.J. Lovell, in giving a reading, made some remarks which were regarded as reflecting on the Parish Council and a former rector, which were strongly resented by many present and vigorous protests made from various parts of the room amid cries of "Rot" and "Put him out". The proceedings came to an abrupt conclusion amid uproar, during which Mr Lovell made a hasty exit from the building. After a time order was restored and the concerts were proceeded with'.

The headstone in Tregony Cemetery of Private Thomas Barnicoat, DCLI. The Author 2004

The headstone in Tregony Cemetery of Private William Thomas Chubb, RASC. The Author 2004

Royal Cornwall Gazette – 22nd November 1917 – Tregoney

'A very successful concert was given on Saturday last by members of the Military Camp at St Anthony. The whole of the items were well rendered, particularly the ventriloquism and conjuring by Sergt Mather, assisted by Miss F. May. There was a crowded house and about £7 will be handed over to the local Work Auxiliary, Red Cross Society. The committee desire to thank those who contributed to the expense and the whole of the takings go to the local Fund without any deduction; also those who gave their services selling tickets, typing programmes and the many other ways. A vote of thanks to the artists was proposed by Mr Real and seconded by Mr E. Grigg'.

Royal Cornwall Gazette – 1st January 1919
Tregoney D.C.M.

'News has been received that Sergt Gordon Davey of the 1st Batt. Royal Irish Fusiliers, an old Tregoney boy, but late residing at Swansea, has won the D.C.M. for great gallantry and devotion to duty in the final fighting against Austria. He has seen much fighting and was wounded in France. Having spent four Christmases abroad, he is expected home shortly, when he hopes to visit his native home'. [The 'Distinguished Conduct Medal' was second only to the Victoria Cross and was awarded for gallantry.]

This photo is of a 1916 charcoal drawing of Private Arthur Burley [Duke of Cornwall's Light Infantry] prior to him joining the fighting. In August 1917 he was killed in action in Flanders.
Unknown source

Royal Cornwall Gazette – 19th
March 1919
Demobilised Solders

'Corpl Richard Beard and Lance Corpl Leonard Real have just arrived home after demobilisation and have received a warm welcome from many friends. Two of the first to join the colours after the outbreak of War, they have not seen their homes for nearly four and a half years, which time has been spent largely in India, Aden, Egypt and Palestine. Both are in splendid health and have luckily come through all the battles without being wounded'.

[N.B. Poor Leonard Real, who was described as "in splendid heath", did not survive for long. See Appendix A, item 23.]

Royal Cornwall Gazette – 16th April 1919
'Our Boys' Fund

'At a meeting of the Committee, held on Saturday last, it was decided to hold a dance in aid of the funds on Easter Monday. Mr. F. Miners, Treasurer, reported a total of about £19 in hand and it is hoped to reach £50, to give each man a souvenir'.

Royal Cornwall Gazette – 20th August 1919 – Missing

'Mr T.M. Leath of the King's Arms Hotel, was notified on Sunday last that his son, Sapper Gordon Leath of the Wireless Telegraphy Dept., had been missing since 20th July last. He had been in Northern Russia since Easter last, and although not 19 years of age until September next, had been in the Army four years. His parents received a letter from him dated 19th July, from which it appeared that the young man had been having some very trying experiences. It is hoped that even now some news may be received of his safety'.

[N.B. Sapper Leath's son recently confirmed that his father had survived the experience. Gordon had been part of the Allied Intervention Force which had been supporting the 'White Russian' forces in the Civil War. After capture by the Bolsheviks, he had been force-marched 500 miles to a Moscow prison. Many of the civilian prisoners with him were executed but he was eventually repatriated after the intervention of the Red Cross.]

Royal Cornwall Gazette – 20th October 1920 – 'Canteen Fund'

'A committee has been appointed by the ex-service men to deal with the quota due to the Parish under the Government scheme in connection with the "Canteen Fund". Capt Welman, M.C., has been elected Chairman; ex -Q.M.S.A. Nicholls, Hon Secretary; and ex–Private E. Julyan, Treasurer. It is suggested that the amount received should form the

The grave of Pte Arthur Burley at Bains Military Cemetery, Dunkerque. His remains were later removed to a military cemetery in Belgium. Unknown source

nucleus of a fund for the provision of a public hall or institute. No parish has made a greater sacrifice during the War than Tregoney. Many of the men returned from all parts of the globe to fight for their King and Country and all would appreciate a comfortable and commodious hall where they could assemble for recreation and social gatherings'.

The Celebrations & the Remembrances

Royal Cornwall Gazette – 22nd January 1919 – War Memorial

At a further public meeting held in the Council School on Sunday evening, Mr James Holman presiding, a resolution rescinding the previous decision to place a tablet in the front wall of the Town Clock and erect an Institute was moved by Mr S. Stephens and carried by a majority of seven. Miss Thompson then moved and Mr T. Holman supported, that a statue be erected in the Square. Miss Thompson asserted that the majority of the relatives of deceased soldiers, including Mrs Welman of Trewarthenick, desired the statue. Miss Elliott said she thought an improvement might be made to the clock. Questioned as to why the decision of the previous meeting had been upset after the Committee had interviewed the relatives and as to whether or not the present decision might be upset at a subsequent meeting, the Chairman said the decision that evening would be carried through. Mr E. Tonkin suggested that the relatives should be given the choice of a few schemes and give their decision in writing, as con-

Peace rejoicing at Tregony on 19th July 1919. A free public tea in Fore Street. The man standing behind the basket is Eldred Grigg. His companion is Sym Stephens.

This poor quality photograph is believed to show the unveiling of the Tregony War Memorial in The Square on 1st Nov 1919.

tradictory reports were received. In a place like Tregoney it seemed a pity to spend from £100 to £150 on a statue when so much good could be done with the money. Those who had served and especially those who had been badly wounded should receive some consideration as well, and no better way of commemorating the dead could be found than doing something to benefit and comfort the living. After considerable discussion it was decided to proceed with the statue in The Square'.

Royal Cornwall Gazette – 19th February 1919 – War Memorial

'At a meeting on Thursday evening, presided over by Mr J. Holman, it was reported that about £105 had been collected towards the War Memorial, including £50 from the Lord Lieutenant, who suggested a Cornish cross; about £8 from a concert, and a similar amount from the Red Cross Auxiliary. The action of a majority of the Committee in persisting on fixing the statue in The Square has been very much criticised, as it is undoubtedly in opposition to the wishes of several of the relatives of deceased soldiers. The first public meeting was practically unanimous in deciding to have an institute as well as a memorial stone and it has been freely rumoured that Mr P. Thomson, Hon Secretary, had received substantial offers of assistance towards an institute, but when questioned on the matter at the meeting he denied the truth of the report. An institute is very badly needed, and a separate committee are determined to spare no effort in order that it may be provided for the benefit of the young men, and particularly those discharged from the Services so maimed as to be unable to indulge in outdoor recreation'.

Royal Cornwall Gazette – 23rd July 1919
Peace Rejoicings – Tregony

'Proceedings in Tregony and district began at 2 p.m. (Saturday 19th) with a procession through the Village headed by the Tregony Victory Band. Juvenile sports ensued, followed by a Free Public Tea. The adults' sports commenced at 7 p.m. followed by a carnival and procession through the Town. There was a display of fireworks and a bonfire at 10.15 p.m., after which dancing was kept up until long after midnight. Prizes were offered for the best decorated houses and the ancient Borough presented a gay appearance'.

Royal Cornwall Gazette – 5th November 1919
Tregoney War Memorial – Unveiled by the Lord Lieutenant
1st November 1919

'The Tregoney War Memorial, which consists of a granite obelisk, on which are inscribed the names of those fallen in the War, and also those who have served in the forces during the conflict, erected on The Square in the centre of the Town on a granite base surrounded by chain palisades, was unveiled on Saturday afternoon by Mr J.C. Williams, Lord Lieutenant of the County, who subscribed £50 towards the funds. Mr Williams was accompanied by Mrs Williams and Miss Williams and amongst the large company present were Capt & Mrs Welman of Trewarthenick. A platform had been erected and Mr W.L. Croggon of Grampound presided. The proceedings commenced with the singing of the hymn, 'O God our Help in Ages Past', followed by a very impressive prayer by the Rev H. Whitehead (Wesleyan Minister). Mr Williams then unveiled the Memorial and in the course of some appropriate remarks, alluded to the fact that Tregoney stood first in the County in the days of voluntary recruiting and had suffered most severely in the number of those who had laid down their lives for their Country.

A vote of thanks to Mr Williams was proposed by Mr Thompson, seconded by Mr Holman and carried with acclaim. Miss Tregunna presided at the harmonium. The Rev F.W. King read the lesson and the proceedings terminated with the singing of the National Anthem. The cost of the Memorial is about £140'.

Royal Cornwall Gazette – 10th November 1920
Tregoney – Armistice Day

'On Sunday afternoon the ex-service men of Tregoney formed a procession near the Church in charge of Capt Hack of Paradise Villa, Veryan, ex-Lieut Clark, ex-Sergt Major Leath and ex-Sergt A. Nicholls of Tregoney. Headed by Tregoney Brass Band, under Mr F. Roberts, they paraded the town, when collections were taken en route for St Dunstan's Hostel for Blind Soldiers. The company afterwards surrounded the monument on the Square which had been erected in memory of those gallant comrades who gave their lives for their country and a very impressive service was held. The band led the singing of appropriate hymns. Mr R.J. Real read the lesson and the Rev F.W. King (Rector) gave a short address on the subject, "They died that we might live". Mr T. Leigh (St Austell) offered prayers and

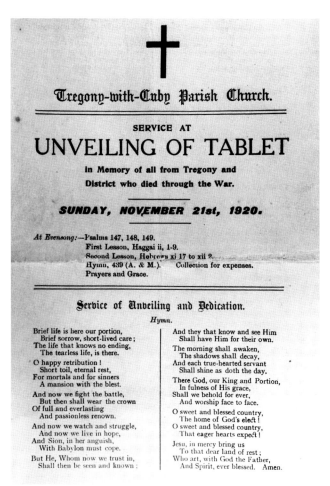

✝

Tregony-with-Cuby Parish Church.

SERVICE AT

UNVEILING OF TABLET

in Memory of all from Tregony and District who died through the War.

SUNDAY, NOVEMBER 21st, 1920.

At Evensong:—Psalms 147, 148, 149.
First Lesson, Haggai ii, 1-9.
Second Lesson, Hebrews xi 17 to xii 9.
Hymn, 439 (A. & M.).   Collection for expenses.
Prayers and Grace.

Service of Unveiling and Dedication.

Hymn.

Brief life is here our portion,
Brief sorrow, short-lived care;
The life that knows no ending,
The tearless life, is there.
O happy retribution!
Short toil, eternal rest,
For mortals and for sinners
A mansion with the blest.
And now we fight the battle,
But then shall wear the crown
Of full and everlasting
And passionless renown.
And now we watch and struggle,
And now we live in hope,
And Sion, in her anguish,
With Babylon must cope.
But He, Whom now we trust in,
Shall then be seen and known;

And they that know and see Him
Shall have Him for their own.
The morning shall awaken,
The shadows shall decay,
And each true-hearted servant
Shall shine as doth the day.
There God, our King and Portion,
In fulness of His grace,
Shall we behold for ever,
And worship face to face.
O sweet and blessed country,
The home of God's elect!
O sweet and blessed country,
That eager hearts expect!
Jesu, in mercy bring us
To that dear land of rest;
Who art, with God the Father,
And Spirit, ever blessed. Amen.

The programme sheet for the service of dedication and unveiling of the Memorial Tablet at Tregony Parish Church, 1920. The Author 2004

ex-Pte John Miners sounded the Reveille and the Last Post. Stanley Leath giving the roll-call on the side drum. The proceedings closed with the National Anthem led by the band. The collection realised £5.5s.'.

Royal Cornwall Gazette – 24th November 1920

'To immortalise the memory of those men from Tregoney and District who gave their lives in the Great War, a mural tablet has been erected in the Parish Church. The unveiling and dedication service was performed on Sunday evening (21st November) by the Bishop of Truro in the presence of a crowded congregation. The ex-servicemen paraded under the command of Capt Hack and ex-Lieut M.K. Clark.

183

The tablet is of white marble, set on slate backing and is inscribed as follows:

"In loving memory of all from this Parish and district who died in the Great War, 1914-1919. Their hope is full of immortality. Erected by the parishioners and friends."

Chapter 15

THE CONCLUSION

So looking back on Tregony in the 1890s, great changes have taken place. All but two of the thatched cottages are gone, so too have the old cobbled pavements, the blocked windows (used to save Window Tax) and all the rows of back-to-back, two-roomed cottages. A new housing estate has been established and the Welfare State has abolished the degrading conditions of the Workhouse and pauperism.

In conclusion, as stated before, this is written mainly for the old Tregonians or those connected with Tregony and I will close with these few lines:

> "Give me a good digestion, Lord
> And also something to digest.
> Give me a healthy body, Lord
> And senses to keep it at its best.
> Give me a mind that is not bored,
> That does not whimper, whine or sigh;
> Don't let me worry overmuch
> About the fussy thing called 'I'.
> Give me a sense of humour, Lord;
> Give me the grace to see a joke,
> To get some happiness in life
> And pass it on to other folk."

Additional Information

Seeking a New World

The prospects of fresh opportunities and plenty of work induced many of the younger, local people to seek their fortunes in the developing New World of the Americas, Africa and Australasia. Some left, never to return, whilst others did their stints and then came back with stories of their adventures. Here are a few newspaper items of the day with some examples of Tregonians who left the old country.

Royal Cornwall Gazette – 31st July 1902

'Mr J. Gerrans, who is now staying at Tregony, his native place, and will be remembered by many of our readers as one of the heroes of the Mafeking siege (South Africa) where his foundry men rendered aid to Baden Powell, in the defence of the little town, has had an interview with Joseph Chamberlain and presented him with a clock made out of a Boer shell which fell into Mafeking'.

Royal Cornwall Gazette – 18th February 1909
A Cornishman's Wedding in South Africa

'A pretty wedding was celebrated at St Monica's Church, Parow, on the 6th, when Mr Harry Jacob, youngest son of the Mr & Mrs John Jacob of Tregoney, was married to Miss Louise Pregnolato of Venice, Italy. The groom, who is a prominent member of the Capetown Metropolitan Fire Brigade, was attended by Mr James Harris of Tregoney as 'best man'.

Royal Cornwall Gazette – 6th October 1920
Tregoney – Gone Abroad

'Mr T.C Woolcock, late clerk to the Parish Council and Overseer, has left for America; and on Friday last Messrs A.J. Harris and R. Olds left for Canada. In addition to these, Messrs S. and W. Ford, Clifford May, W. Lidgey and G. Furze have crossed the Atlantic within the last two months, and S. Gay has gone to the Malay States. All these men have served in the Forces and it is a matter for regret (writes a correspondent) that they should have to leave their native town for foreign countries in order to obtain work at good living wages. Not only has the Prime Minister failed to make England a fit place for heroes to live in, but the glorious Free Trade system of the country has now not kept energetic young men from rushing off to highly protected countries where, in spite of what we have been told to the contrary, labour conditions are vastly superior to those found at home'.

Royal Cornwall Gazette – 16th June 1920
Tregony Presentations

'Members of the Tregoney Football Club on Thursday presented Mr Clifford May, late Captain of the team, with a silver wristwatch and Mr George Furze with a silver hairbrush set, in recognition of services rendered to the Club on their leaving for America. Both men had seen much active service and all wished them well in their ventures overseas'.

Extracts of a letter written[1] in the 1920s by Chas. W. Ford of Michigan, U.S.A to the May family in Nebraska (all ex-Tregonians) :

15879 Normandy Ave
Detroit

"*Today I got a letter from home with your address in it so you see I am on the job.*

I have just arrived in Detroit from a trip to Tregoney, I had ten weeks there and I found all your people in fairly good spirits considering the conditions in England at the time. I had a real good time home there and saw quite a lot of Will and his wife and family, a fine family. The boys are a fine lot of young men and a credit to a lot of others I know at Tregoney and the girls all look well.

We now have a crowd in Detroit from Tregoney. I have two brothers (Will and Steve) and there are three Lidgeys (Steve Lidgey's two sons and Edgar), Janie's son (Dick), and Jane May's son (Clifford), and William James Greet's daughter (Irene), and Frank Miner's two sons, so you see there is a little Tregoney in Detroit. We are often together once a week and all work for the same firm – Ford Motor Co. Some name, some place, but all the same we get good pay. Most of us get $7.20 a day, but we have to work and we have to do that any place. Everyone here enjoys good health and is contented I believe.

Now all the boys wish you and all others all good health. I live with the Lidgey boys, all board together.

I am yours etc, an old Tregoney boy – Chas W. Ford."

Things did turn rather sour for some of the emigrants in the 1930s.

Here is an extract from a letter[2], dated December 9th 1934, written by William Thomas Barnicoat in Des Moines, Iowa, to his sister, Mrs Fanny Dowrick, in Tregony:

"*I got a letter from Steve Lidgey from Ohio. I was away from Des Moines so I never answered his letter. Well Fanny things are awful out here, thousands are out of work and I have been roaming around the country the last two years, picking work, here and there. I always look for Des Moines my own town. We have got lots of snow and I think its going to be a hard winter.*

Well I must close with the best and fondest love. Best of wishes to all, Merry Christmas.

From yours
W.T. Barnicoat."

William Thomas Barnicoat left Tregony in about 1908, aged 25 yrs. and travelled to Canada. On the 11th April 1909 he entered the U.S.A. at Port Huron, Michigan via the Grand Trunk Railway from Tilsonburg, Canada and settled in Des Moines, Iowa. He was a general handyman by trade but he never made his fortune. He died unmarried and living alone in rented accommodation in Des Moines in 1963. William never visited England again but he did keep in contact with some of his old friends in America.

In 1995, I visited Des Moines and located Willie's unmarked grave. I marked the site with an inscribed plaque which read: "In Memory of William Thomas BARNICOAT, died Des Moines, 10th July 1963, aged 80 years. – Reunited with his kinfolk from Tregony, Cornwall, England. October1995. Frank Grigg (great nephew)." I dampened the soil with water collected from St Cuby's Well and I sprinkled earth from his homeland.

'TREGONY HAPPENINGS'

An example of the weekly rhyming newsletter taken from the Royal Cornwall Gazette – 16th November 1921. The writer is believed to have been Mr E.W. Tonkin. This item was a mix of light-hearted local banter together with comments on the serious social needs of the time.

"On Saturday at Grampound our team lost another game;
And until they alter methods it will always be the same.
In George, Mark and Aaron there is football still, no doubt,
And it would greatly help the youngsters if they would again turn out.

The Men's and Women's Institutes did what we think was right
In getting up a Social for our Band on Friday night;
For the Band is always ready to respond to any call,
And deserves to be supported by our people,
One and all.

They must have a new drum for Charlie or he may get out of tune;
And all the E Flats will be B Flats unless they are replaced soon.
Provided with new equipment they would give us of their best,
And perhaps next year at Bugle become the champions of the West.

England was to be fit for heroes, so our old friend Lloyd George said;
But there are thousands now in Cornwall even short of daily bread.
After the crisis we have passed through no cupboard should be bare,
For there is plenty in old England for all to have a share.

Those, who through war conditions, made their little pile
Ought now to be proud and happy to help others o'er the stile;
Yet we hear of many who no sympathy have felt,
But they can't take their money with them, and if they did, 'twould melt."

Tregony Infants Class of 1921-22.

(Back row, l-r) Gus Burley, Dennis Harris, Ritchie Bullen, u/k boy, Winston Bilkey, Anthony Wheeler, George Barnicoat, William Moyses.
(Centre row, l-r) Gordon Gay, Leo Lidgey, Bert Blackler, Evelyn Parsons, Hilda Clemow, Violet Grose?, Vivie Blackler, Roy Hawkins.
(Front row, l-r) Janet Pearce, Joyce Harris, Lillian Barnicoat, Queenie Nicholls, May Northcott, Minnie Greet, Amy Davis, Margaret Greet, Morvie Cutler and Betty Cloke.

The Tregony Infants Class of 1921~2

What was to be the destiny of these little ones? Young faces gazing wistfully to a brighter future. Meanwhile, we glance back at the past and understand the reality.

References

1   Letter from Charles W. Ford in USA dated 1920 – copy with the Author.
2   Letter from William T. Barnicoat in USA dated 1930s – copy with the Author

Appendix A

Service Personnel Killed in the First World War

1914 –1919

The following, is a record of the personal details of local men and one woman who died as result of the Great War. Data was compiled from various sources including The Commonwealth War Graves Commission, local newspapers, War Memorials and local knowledge.

Franklin Grigg

1. BARNICOAT Edwin: Private, No. 34931 of the 1st/4th Battalion of the Duke of Cornwall's Light Infantry who was killed in action on the 27th April 1918 whilst fighting the Turks at a Village called Rafat, in what was then Palestine. He was buried in Ramleh War Cemetery. He enlisted at Bodmin, Cornwall in 1916.

Royal Cornwall Gazette – 16th May 1918 – "Mrs BARNICOAT of Bridgend, Lostwithiel (formerly of Tregoney) has lost a second son, Private Eddie BARNICOAT."

Edwin was the eighth child of Thomas & Celia Ann BARNICOAT of Tregony and he was a single man. He was born at Tregony on the 21st April 1897. His death is also recorded on the War Memorial at St Necton's Chapel near Lostwithiel. His family had moved to Bridgend, Lostwithiel after the death of Edwin's brother, Thomas, in 1916.

2. BARNICOAT Thomas: Private, No. 17794 of the 7th Battalion of the Duke of Cornwall's Light Infantry, died as result of wounds received whilst on active service in Flanders. His death took place at a London hospital on 9th December 1916. He was buried on the 12th December in the cemetery beside Tregony Parish Church.

Royal Cornwall Gazette – 14th December 1916 – "It was with much regret that we received the news of the death on Saturday of Private Tommy BARNICOAT, D.C.L.I., in a London hospital, as result of wounds received at the front. The poor young fellow had a terrible experience on the battlefield at Combles, Somme, having been shot in the spine and lying on the ground unable to move a hand or foot for two nights and a day before rescued. At his express wish he will be buried in the cemetery of his native parish."

Thomas was the seventh child of Thomas & Celia Ann BARNICOAT of Tregony. He was born at Tregony on the 26th January 1895 and was an elder brother of Edwin, (see No 1 above).

3. BEARD Frederick: Private, No 10518 of the 7th Battalion of the Duke of Cornwall's Light Infantry, died of wounds on the 16th August 1917, aged 25 yrs, whilst fighting in Flanders. He was buried in the Mensing Military Cemetery, Poperinge, West Vlaanderen, Belgium.

Royal Cornwall Gazette – 1st November 1917 – "Pte Arthur MINERS who has been on home leave has been through some of the most severe fighting and has had some marvellous escapes. On one occasion he with a comrade, carried to the casualty station Pte BEARD, son of Mr W.H.*BEARD of Ladock (who by the way is also an old Tregoney boy), under heavy fire, but unfortunately BEARD died almost immediately. On returning to their post, Pte MINERS and his mate were standing close together when the latter was struck in the neck by a shell and killed instantly."

[* This appears to be a mistake as the father's initials were A.H.]

Frederick was the son of Albert Henry & Mary BEARD of Ladock, Cornwall and he was born at Tregony. He would have been listed on the Ladock Memorial.

4. BEARD William John: Sergeant, No. 8570, 3rd Regiment, South African Infantry, who died, aged 33 yrs, on Thursday 20th September 1917 whilst fighting in France in the 3rd Battle of Ypres. He is remembered with honour at Ypres (Menin Gate) Memorial, Leaper, West Vlaanderen, Belgium.

Royal Cornwall Gazette – 11th October 1917 – "We very much regret to have to add another name to the Roll of Honour for Tregoney District – 12 from the Town have met their death in war, excluding Pte Jack COLEMAN reported missing. The latest victim is Sgt W.J. BEARD (S.A.I.), eldest son of Mr Richard BEARD, Fore Street, who was killed on the 20th ult. Sgt BEARD joined the forces in South Africa and previous to going to that country was a regular playing member of the local football team, and a member of the brass band. He was a thorough sportsman, and his death is regretted by all who knew him. The following letter has been received by his Mother from Capt L.W. THOMLINSON: "On behalf of my Company, allow me to convey to you our deepest sympathy in the loss of your very gallant son. He fell whilst we were attacking an enemy strongpoint on the 20th inst. I was particularly struck with his bearing during the fight, he was quite unconcerned and was a fine example to the men around him. We buried him next day on the spot where he fell and a cross was erected. I deeply sympathise with your bereavement but there is consolation and, may I say it, pride in the knowledge that you were permitted to be the mother of such a brave lad, who made the supreme sacrifice in the cause of liberty and right."

William John (known as Jack) was the son of Richard & Mary BEARD of Myrtle View, Tregony, Cornwall and a brother to Lily, Daisy, Gladys, Fred, Richard, Louis and Sid.

5. BUCKINGHAM Reginald John James: Private, No. 20279 of the 6th Battalion of the Somerset Light Infantry, died on the 23rd March 1918, aged 27 yrs, of wounds received. He is buried in the Noyon New British Cemetery, Oise, France.

Reggie was the son of J.& S. BUCKINGHAM of Ruan Lanihorne, Cornwall, and the husband of Rhona GREET (formerly BUCKINGHAM) of Faircross, Grampound.

Royal Cornwall Gazette – 28th March 1918 – "Mrs BUCKINGHAM of Cuby Cottage, Tregoney has received notification that her husband, Bandsman Reginald BUCKINGHAM, has been wounded but is progressing favourably."

Royal Cornwall Gazette – 16th May 1918 – "Mrs BUCKINGHAM, Tregoney, has received a telegram from the War Office, that her husband (Bandsman Reg J.J. BUCK-INGHAM) died on the 23rd March of wounds received in action on 21st, at the 46th Casualty Clearing Station, France. Bandsman BUCKINGHAM was reported wounded on March 25th and up to a few days ago 'no further information' was forthcoming as to his condition or whereabouts, which kept the family in dreadful suspense. Joining the forces three years ago he had been in France about two and a half years and when on leave in February was at the St Quentin sector, which explains a great deal. Letters have been received from fellow bandsmen throwing light on the circumstances that led to his death. One of them wrote: 'Old Fritz kept coming over in his planes and flying low, turned his machine guns on us. After this he started shelling, and the Battalion having gone ahead, the Band were ordered up to support two companies of Scots, with the result that one was killed, one missing and three wounded.'

Deceased was the elder son of Mr J. BUCKINGHAM, the late popular Bandmaster of Tregoney Band, and was well known in musical circles locally, forming one of the BUCKINGHAM family who had assisted so frequently in pre-war days at concerts."

6. BURLEY Arthur: Private, No. 26743 of the 10th Battalion of the Duke of Cornwall's Light Infantry, who on the 16th August 1917, at the age of 27 yrs, was killed in action in Flanders. His body was buried at the Ramscappelle Road Military Cemetery, Nieuwpoort, West Vlaanderen, Belgium.

Royal Cornwall Gazette – 30th August 1917 – "Pte Arthur BURLEY, second son of

Mr Charles & Mary BURLEY of Castle View, Tregoney, was killed in action on the 15th instant. He was struck by a shell and death was instantaneous. He had been serving in the D.C.L.I. since April 1916 and went to France in the first week of January. Mr BURLEY'S other two sons are serving."

7. CARHART Percy: Private, No. 36117 of the 1st Battalion of the Duke of Cornwall's Light Infantry, was killed in action on the 30th October 1917 in Flanders. A record of his name can be found at the Tyne Cot Memorial, Zonnebeke, West Vlaanderen, Belgium.

Royal Cornwall Gazette – 29th November 1917 – Listed as killed – "Percy CARHART, D.C.L.I., aged 19, of Scarcewater nr. Tregony."

Percy was born at St Kew, Cornwall, but at the time of his enlistment at Bodmin, his address was given as Tregony. He was the son of Mrs E. CARHART of Scarcewater Hill, St Stephen, Cornwall.

8. CARHART Reginald T.: Private, No. 200815 of the 2nd/4th Battalion of the Duke of Cornwall's Light Infantry, who died in India on the 29th October 1918 and is buried at the Delhi War Cemetery in India.

Royal Cornwall Gazette – 5th February 1919 – "In memory of Private Reginald CARHART, aged 21 yrs, the eldest son of Mr & Mrs Marcina CARHART of Barwick Farm, Cuby, Tregoney, who died at Delhi, India on October 29th 1918 of pneumonia following influenza. Deceased joined the D.C.L.I. just after the outbreak of war and went to India with the Territorials about four years ago. He had been looking to rejoining the family circle at an early date and belated news of his demise came as a great shock to the family."

Reggie was born at St Kew in 1898 and enlisted in the Army at Bodmin.

9. CHUBB William Thomas: Private, SS/23017 of the Army Service Corp, who died on Monday 13th March 1916 of broncho-pneumonia at the Cambridge Hospital, Aldershot, and who is buried in the old Cemetery beside Tregony Parish Church.

The Burial Register records that he was 48 years old, a labourer in the A.S.C. and that his home address was The Cambridge, Tregony. The Tregony School Records indicate that William was married and had four young daughters. Prior to the war he had been a farm labourer by trade.

10. COLEMAN John Clyma: Private, No. 202141 of the 2nd Battalion of the Royal Berkshire Regiment, who died, aged 34 yrs, during the 3rd Battle of Ypres, in France, on Thursday 16th August 1917. His name is listed at the Tyne Cot Memorial for missing soldiers at Zonnebeke, West Vlaanderen, Belgium

Royal Cornwall Gazette – 20th September 1917 – "Mrs COLEMAN of Tregoney has received notice from the War Office, that her husband, Pte John COLEMAN has been missing since the 16th instant. They have been married about 12 months."

John, who was born at Perranzabuloe, Cornwall, was the husband of Harriet Beatrice COLEMAN (neé ROBERTS) of Tregony, Cornwall. They were married on the 22 nd April, 1916 at Truro.

11. CUTLER Frank: 2nd Lieutenant of the 14th Battalion of the Durham Light Infantry, died on Monday 18th September 1916 whilst fighting in France and is buried at the A.I.F. Burial Ground at Flers, Somme. Frank was the husband of Hettie CUTLER of Tregony, Cornwall.

Royal Cornwall Gazette – 5th October 1916 – "Lieut Frank CUTLER – Killed in Action. Mrs CUTLER of Agar Place, Tregoney has received a letter from Capt. BLOY, Durham Light Infantry as follows:- Dear Mrs Cutler, I am sorry to have to tell you that your husband, 2nd Lieut F. CUTLER, was killed in action on the 18th September. He was shot by a sniper and died instantly. We in the Company miss him very much and he was a very valuable Officer. Please accept the sympathy of all officers and men." The article went on to say, "Lieut CUTLER was a native of Birmingham and served for 15 yrs in the D.C.L.I. He was for some years stationed at Bodmin, where he held Sergeant's rank and where he was extremely popular. He rose up position by smartness and ability and was expecting further promotion when his career was cut short. Mrs CUTLER is the daughter of Mr W.H. JULIAN of Tregoney, who has five sons-in-law serving, one of whom was a Warrant Officer and lost his life in the Battle of Jutland. Deep sympathy is felt with Mrs CUTLER and her children."

12. FUGLER William George: Chief Armourer (Pensioner), No. 127754, Royal Navy was killed on New Year's Day, 1915, when *H.M.S. Formidable* was lost at sea. At 2.30 a.m. the battleship, whilst on exercises, was torpedoed by a German submarine (U.24) and sank in 180 feet of water about 37 miles off the Devon coast. Only 199 men were saved out of a complement of about 750. He has no known grave. His name is remembered with honour on the Portsmouth Naval Memorial.

William was born at Tregony in about 1864, one of the children of James & Jane Fugler. They lived at Rosehill, Cornelly. In 1889 he married Emma Jane Southwell at Portsea. Hants. It is probable that he had already joined the R.N. by that time. In 1901 Emma and two sons, Frederick and William, were living in Portsmouth. This remained the family home up until the death of William.

13. GREET Caleb: Private, No SS/13944, 18th Labour Coy; Army Service Corps, died on Friday 13th August 1915 whilst on active service near Gallipoli. His name is listed on the Helles Memorial at Gallipoli, Turkey, which contains names of the Allied Forces who died in the campaign.

Royal Cornwall Gazette – 19th August 1915 – "British Transport – Torpedoed. – The British Transport ship, *Royal Edward*, was sunk by an enemy submarine in the Aegean last Saturday evening. The ship had on board 32 military officers and 1350 troops in addition to a ship's crew of 220. It is known that a party of men of the 18th Labour Munitions Company, A.S.C, were on board and word has been received that some 86 of them have been saved. The list of names is still awaited."

West Briton newspaper – 9th Sept 1915 – "Mr Caleb GREET, one of the victims of the *Royal Edward*, who joined the Labourer Force only three months ago was well known throughout Tregoney and district, having run a conveyance regularly between Truro and St Austell."

Caleb lived at Fore Street, Tregoney. He was married to Eliza Maud GREET (neé PRING) and they had five children. He was born at Gwennap, Cornwall, in 1860.

14. HENWOOD Harry: Private, No. 41161 of the 4th Battalion of the Worcestershire Regiment, who died, on the 30th November 1917, aged 18 yrs, whilst in action against the Germans in the Battle of Cambrai, France. He has no known grave. His name is listed on the Cambrai Memorial at Louvernal, Nord, France.

Royal Cornwall Gazette – 10th January 1918 – "We regret to report that a Tregoney lad is reported missing, Private Harry HENWOOD."

Harry was the son of Mrs Mary Ellen HENWOOD, widow, of the Cambridge, Tregony.

15. LEAN Reginald: Driver, No. 109645 of the 377th Battery, 169th Bde, the Royal Field Artillery, who died, aged 20 yrs, on Wednesday 6th February 1918 whilst on active service in Aisne, France. He is buried at the Montescourt – Lizerolles Communal Cemetery, Aisne.

Royal Cornwall Gazette – 14th February 1918 – "We regret to report that another Tregoney lad has been called upon to make the supreme sacrifice in war. Mrs LEAN of New Road Cottage, Tregoney received on Sunday a letter from Lieut J. SMITH R.F.A., informing her that her son, Driver R. LEAN, was killed on the 5th by a bomb. His death was instantaneous. Driver LEAN was 20 years of age and had been in France about nine months. Much sympathy is felt for Mrs LEAN, who was expecting her son to come home about the time she received the sad intelligence. Deceased was considered to be one of the smartest young soldiers that left the location and his death brings to 14 the number of local soldiers who have given their lives for their Country, in addition to which three are reported as missing."

Reggie was the son of Bessie LEAN of Tregony, Cornwall. He was born at St Stephen in Brannell but spent most of his life in Tregony.

16. **LYNDON Edwin Philip**: Private, No. 29122 of the 1st Battalion of the Hampshire Regiment, who died, aged 18 yrs, on Thursday 24th October 1918 whilst on active service in France. He was buried at Monchaux Communal Cemetery, Nord, France.

Royal Cornwall Gazette – 13th November 1918 – Tregony & District – "Much sympathy is felt with Mr & Mrs R. LYNDON who have just lost a second son at the front. Pte E. LYNDON had only been in France a few weeks before his death."

Edwin was born at Probus in 1900 and was the son of Robert & Susan Mary LYNDON of Probus, Cornwall. His older, half-brother, Harry, had previously been killed in action in 1916. At the time of Edwin's death, his widowed father was living at Probus with Jane LYNDON (Edwin's grandmother). Edwin is also listed on the Probus War Memorial.

17. **LYNDON Henry**: Private, No. 12964 of the 8th Battalion of the Duke of Cornwall's Light Infantry, who was killed in action on Sunday 12th November 1916 whilst fighting on the Doiran front in Greece. He was buried at the Karasouli Military Cemetery in Greece."

Royal Cornwall Gazette – 23rd November 1916 – Roll of Honour. – "News has been received of the death in action at Salonika on Nov 12th of Harry LYNDON, 30, D.C.L.I., son of Mr Robert LYNDON of Freewater, Probus."

Harry, as he was known, was born in Montgomery, Wales, in 1887. He was the son of Robert & Elizabeth Ann LYNDON. After the death of Elizabeth Ann, Robert came back to the Probus/Tregony area in about 1898 with his sons. Harry enlisted at Truro, Cornwall. At the time of Harry's death, Robert the father had remarried and was living at Freewater, Probus. Harry's younger, half-brother, Edwin, was later to become a war victim when he was killed in 1918. Both brothers are also named on the Probus War Memorial.

18. **MAY Richard John**: Private, No. 241342 of the 6th Battalion, Queen's Own (Royal West Kent Regiment), who died on Sunday 2nd December 1917, aged 22 yrs,

whilst fighting nr. Cambrai, France. He is buried at St Aubert British Cemetery, Nord, France."

Royal Cornwall Gazette – 28th February 1918 – Roll of Honour.

"We deeply regret to have to add the fifteenth name to the Roll of Honour for the Tregoney district. Mr W.H. Miners MAY received on the 24th instant, information from the War Office that his eldest son, Private Richard John MAY, 6th Royal West Kent Regiment, died in a field hospital at St Hilaire (whilst a prisoner of war) on December 2nd, 1917. His death was the result of wounds received in action and he was buried in the cemetery by the St Hilaire to Quievy Road. Pte MAY had been missing since the Battle of Cambrai on November 29th, 1917. He had only been on the front about two months and was 22 years of age. Mr Miners MAY had himself served in France in the Labour Section and has 2 other sons serving."

Richard, a single man, was born in Tregony in September 1895, one of the sons of William Henry Miners. & Nettie MAY of Fore Street, Tregony, Cornwall.

19. MOUNTSTEPHEN(S) William Nicholas: Private, No. 22595 of the 7th Battalion of the Duke of Cornwall's Light Infantry, who died aged 19 yrs, on the 13th April 1916 of wounds received whilst fighting in Flanders. He is buried at the Lijssenthoek Military Cemetery at Poperinge, West Vlaanderen, Belgium."

Nicholas, as he was known, was born at Tregony on the 16th January 1897, one of a large family of Solomon & Kate MOUNTSTEPHEN of Tregony.

20. NOBLE Robert Curnow: Private, No. 18598 of the 1st Battalion of the Duke of Cornwall's Light Infantry, was killed in action in Flanders on Sunday 4th July 1915. He was buried in the First D.C.L.I. Cemetery, the Bluff Leaper, West Vlaanderen, Belgium.

Robert was born at Gulval, near Penzance, Cornwall in 1897. At the time he enlisted into the Army at Bodmin, his address was given as Trewarthenick House, which is a large Country Estate situated at Cornelly near to Tregony. It is probable that he was employed on the estate.

21. PATRICK Lilian Pretoria: A Clerical Staff Worker of the Queens Mary's Army Auxiliary Corp who died in London, aged 18 yrs, on Sunday 27th October 1918. She is remembered and honoured at Lambeth (Tooting) Cemetery, London, in a wall screen.

Royal Cornwall Gazette – 30th October 1918 – "The news of the death of Miss Lilian Pretoria PATRICK, second daughter of Police Sergeant & Mrs PATRICK of

Tregoney, which took place at Mildway Hospital, London on Saturday last, came as a great surprise to everyone and deep sympathy is felt with the parents and family in their sad and sudden bereavement. Deceased, who was well known in the district, was only 18 years of age and was connected with the Church Choir and Sunday School prior to leaving home in August last to take up work in connection with Q.M.W.A.A.C. (Clerical Section). The parents received a letter on Saturday morning to the effect that she had been removed to hospital suffering from influenza and pneumonia, and Mrs PATRICK at once left for London, only to find on her arrival that her daughter had passed away."

Lilian was born at Bodmin, Cornwall, on the 13th July 1900. She was the daughter of William and Lucy PATRICK. Her father was a Police Sergeant of the Cornwall Constabulary who was posted to Tregony in about 1914. Lilian and her brother attended Tregony School until she left the district in 1916. At the time of her death her parents were living in Fore Street, St Columb, Cornwall.

22. PETERS Alfred: Private, 6/2242, aged 39 years of the 2nd Battalion of the Canterbury Regiment of the New Zealand Expeditionary Force was killed in action in France on the 30th May 1916. He was buried at the Bailleul Communal Cemetery Extension, (Nord).

Royal Cornwall Gazette – 23rd November 1916 – Tregoney.

"Private Alfred PETERS, a native of Tregoney, who came all the way from New Zealand to fight for his Country at the Dardanelles, was killed in France."

Alfred who was born in Tregony in 1877 was the second son of William & Mary PETERS who lived at Tregony.

23. REAL Leonard John: Leonard was born at Portscatho, Cornwall, on the 14th August 1891, one of the sons of Richard & Eliza REAL. In 1891 the family moved to Tregony where the father took up the position of Headmaster in the Village School. They all resided in the Schoolhouse which adjoins the School. Leonard became a carpenter and stayed at Tregony.

West Briton Newspaper – 30th September 1920 – "Ex-Sappers Death – After a painful illness the death took place at Schoolhouse, Tregoney on Thursday of Mr Leonard REAL, aged 29, son of Mr R.J. REAL, headmaster of Tregoney Council School. The deceased, who enlisted in the Army in August 1914, served in India, Aden and Palestine with the 1st/4th Duke of Cornwall's Light Infantry and was subsequently transferred to the Royal Engineers. He was demobilised about 18 months ago but afterwards broke down in health. He underwent a serious operation at the Royal

Cornwall Infirmary a short time since, became worse and his death was not unexpected. He was a member of the Church Choir and Tregoney Football Club and took a keen interest in all matters of Village life. This funeral took place on Monday and was largely attended."

He was buried in the Cemetery beside Tregony Parish Church and the headstone bears the text: "In loving memory of **– Leonard John REAL** – the beloved son of – **R.J. & E. REAL** – who died at School House Tregoney – Sept 24 th 1920 after serving 4 years – in the Great War aged 29 years."

24. SPEAR Christopher John: The *Royal Cornwall Gazette* on 1st July 1915 reported that "Christopher SPEAR from Tregony has been wounded in action."

Royal Cornwall Gazette – 21st March 1918 – Roll of Honour. "We regret to record the death of Mr Christopher John SPEAR of Cuby Cottage, Tregoney, which took place on Sunday last. Mr SPEAR enlisted in the Duke of Cornwall's Light Infantry about three years ago and in the following June he was very badly gassed at Ypres. After spending a considerable time in hospital he was invalided out of the service and got worse. His deaths brings to 16 the total number of war victims for the Tregoney District. Much sympathy is felt with the widow and Mrs SPEAR (mother) and family. The widow is a daughter of Mr W.H. JULIAN, who has had three sons-in-law killed in action."

The *Royal Cornwall Gazette* on 20th Sept 1917 stated that "The generosity of Mr J.C. WILLIAMS to the poor of Tregony has been well marked and his latest gift is a large water-proof canvas shelter to Mr E. TONKIN for the use of an ex-soldier suffering from consumption through being gassed and requires outdoor treatment. The tent will be available for further cases. The cost was £10."

In the 1990s, Christopher John's son, Ronald SPEAR, recalled that when he was a boy, on warm summer days, several of the family would carry his father (Christopher) in his bed up into the fields behind the Church in order that he could enjoy the sun and breathe the fresh air.

Christopher was born at Gorran, Cornwall, on the 24th Feb 1887. In 1915, his younger brother, James, was killed in action in Belgium.

25. SPEAR James Henry: Private, No. 18346 of the 1st Battalion of the Duke of Cornwall's Light Infantry, aged 21 yrs, was killed in action in Flanders on Wednesday 5th May 1915. He is buried at the First D.C.L.I. Cemetery, the Bluff, Leaper, West Vlaanderen, Belgium.

Royal Cornwall Gazette – 13th May 1915 – "Private James H. SPEAR, D.C.L.I., son of Mrs SPEAR of Stanbury Row, Tregony, was killed in action on the 5th inst. His brothers Joseph and William are in the army."

Royal Cornwall Gazette – 8th July 1915 – Roll of Honour. "Mrs SPEAR of Tregoney (mother) received the following letter from the Company Commander. About 9 am on the 5th the Germans commenced using poison gas immediately on our left. My orders were to open heavy fire on German trenches opposite to keep them from occupying the trenches gassed. In doing so your son was shot through the head and lingered about a quarter of an hour, being unconscious the whole time. He was buried in the Battalion Graveyard and given the last rites. A cross bearing his name has been erected. His loss was greatly felt by officers and men of his Company. He was well liked, a brave and thorough soldier."

James was unmarried and the son of John (late) & Caroline SPEAR of Tregony. James was born at Gorran, Cornwall, on the 8th March 1894. His brother Christopher died as result of the effects of the War in 1918.

26. TONKIN Harry: Sergeant, No. 10860 of the 11th Battalion of the Queen's (Royal West Surrey Regiment) died, aged 21 yrs, on Friday 19th October 1917 from wounds received in action in France. He was buried at the Zuydcoote Military Cemetery, Nord, France."

Royal Cornwall Gazette – 1st November 1917 – "The news of the death of Sgt Harry TONKIN, youngest son of Mr J.H TONKIN, grocer of Tregoney, as a result of wounds received in action on the 19th October last, has cast a gloom over the whole district, where deceased was universally liked and respected, and the deepest sympathy is felt with the bereaved parents and other relatives. Sgt TONKIN, Royal West Surreys, had been in France for 19 months and had been through most of the severe fighting. He was held in high esteem by the officers and men of his regiment. A memorial service was held in the Parish Church on Wednesday evening. He was for a number of years connected with the Church choir and Sunday School. The death of Sgt TONKIN brings the number of brave dead for the Tregoney district to 14."

He was the son of Mr Joseph Henry & Mary Edith TONKIN of Tregony, Cornwall. Harry was born at Tregony on the 26th November 1895.

27. VINCENT James Henry: Private, No.3204 of the 1st Battalion of the Duke of Cornwall's Light Infantry, was killed in action in France on Saturday 13th January 1917. His body was buried at the Ovillers Military Cemetery, Somme, France.

Harry, as he was known, was one of the sons of William Thomas & Mary VINCENT of Coronation Terrace, Tregony. He was born at Cuby, Tregony, on the 10th May

1895 and grew up in the Village.

28. WARNE John Percy: Private, No. 44921 of the 4th Battalion of the Duke of Cornwall's Light Infantry, died on Monday 24th February 1919, and is remembered with honour at Perranzabuloe (St Piran) Churchyard.

Royal Cornwall Gazette – 5th March 1919 – Tregoney. "Much sympathy is felt with Mr John & Mrs Alice WARNE at Tregonhayne, and their family, in the loss of their elder son, Cadet Percy WARNE of the Royal Air Force, who died at the Military Hospital, Londonderry on the 24th ult. Deceased was only 18 years old."

He was a brother to the late Mr Charles Warne of Tregonhayne, Tregony.

29. WELMAN Henry Bolt: Lieutenant, *H.M.S. Victory*, Royal Marine Light Infantry, who died, aged 23 yrs, on Monday 13th November 1916. He was buried at Mailly Wood Cemetery, Somme, France.

Royal Cornwall Gazette – 23rd November 1916 – "Lieut Henry Bolt WELMAN, R.M.L.I., whose death in action is recorded, was the third son of Mr Henry Acton WELMAN & Mrs Mary Laetitia WELMAN of Trewarthenick. He was 23 years of age. After being a student at Camborne School of Mines he obtained a Commission in the R.M.L.I. and went through the Gallipoli Campaign."

Appendix B

Servicemen who survived the First World War

This is a roll-call of the Tregony and District men who fought in the First World War and who did survive. Copied from The War Memorial in the Square at Tregony. Further details have been added by the Author:

BAKER H.	Harry – born 6th April 1891
BARNICOAT A.	Aaron – born 26 Sept 1880 Tregony
BARNICOAT E.	Edward – born 16 June 1888 Gorran
BARNICOAT J.	Joseph – born 1896 Tregony
BARNICOAT L.	Leonard – born about 1897
BEARD A.C.	Albert Charles – born about 1880
BEARD E.	Ernest – born 23 Aug 1890
BEARD F.D.	Frederick
BEARD L.A.	Lewis Arthur – born 3 Jan 1893
BEARD R.L.	Richard Leonard
BUCKINGHAM N.P.	Norman Peter – born 6 June 1895 Ruan Lanihorne
BURLEY C.	Charles – born about 1887
BURLEY L.	Lewis – born 10 Jan 1893
BURLEY R.J.	Richard John – born about 1887
BURLEY S.	-
CARBIS J.	James
CONGDON S.	Sydney – born 11 April 1896 Plymouth
DAVEY H.	Herbert – born 10 May 1882
DAVEY P.	Percy – born 27 Aug 1899 Tregony
DOWRICK A.	Alphonso – born 12 Dec 1884 Tregony
DOWRICK F.	Frederick – born 24 June 1892 Tregony
DUSTOW S.	Sydney – born 7 Oct 1899 Veryan
ELLIOTT C.H.	Charles Herbert – born 6 March 1880
EVANS J.C.	John Charles – born 16 Nov 1898 Tregony

FORD C.W.E.	Charles William Eplett – 12 April 1889 Tregony
FORD S.	Stephen
FORD S.J.	Stephen James – born 16 Jan 1895 St Ewe
FORD W.R.	William – born 3 Oct 1889 Veryan
FURZE E.E.	Edward E. – born 20 March 1890 Tregony
FURZE F.J.	Frederick John – born 6 Oct 1886 Tregony
FURZE G.S.	George S. – born 24 May 1897 Tregony
FURZE W.J.	William Joseph – born 17 May 1885 Tregony
FURZE W.S.	Wallace Stanley – born 17 Oct 1891 Tregony
GAY J.S.	Stanley – born 11 - Sept 1886 Tregony
GREET A.V.	Alfred V. – born 19 June 1897
HARRIS A.J.	Albert John – born 7 April 1899 Tregony
HARRIS W.C.	William Charles – born 24 Nov 1894 St Austell
HENWOOD A.	Alfred – born 27 Feb 1900 Tregony
HENWOOD W.	William – born 13 April 1897 Tregony
JACOB M.	Mark – born Sept 1883
JULYAN A.E.	Albert Ernest – born 7 June 1883 Reskivers
JULYAN T.	Thomas – born 24 July 1884 Tregony
LEAN C.	Charles – born 17 March 1894 St Stephen
LIDGEY E.	Edgar – born 14 July 1889 Truro
LIDGEY S.W.	Stephen W. – born about 1899
MATTHEWS J.H.	James Henry – born 5 Sept 1899 Tregony
MAY A.J.	Arthur James – born 2 April 1892
MAY A.L.	Alwyn Llewellyn – born 12 Sept 1890
MAY C.H.	Clifford Harold – born 30 March 1898
MAY H.	Harry 'Yank' – born 6 Nov 1890
MAY M.	Michael – born 10 Feb 1885 Tregony
MAY P.	Philip – born 30 Nov 1899
MAY R.J.	Richard John – born about 1895
MAY V.	Victor – born 25 April 1897 Tregony
MINERS A.	Arthur – born 12 Sept 1895 Tregony
MINERS J.	John – born 29 April 1900 Tregony
MOUNSTEPHEN S.	Solomon – born 25 Dec 1890 St Michael Penkevil
NICHOLLS A.E.	Arthur Edmund – born 9 Aug 1879 Tregony
PELLOW F.	-
PERDUE B.F.	-
PETHICK A.E.	Arthur Evelyn – born 1 Aug 1890 Sticker

REAL L.J.	Leonard John – born 14 Aug 1891 Portscatho
ROBERTS H.E.	Hugh Eplett – born about 1888
ROBERTS W.J.	William James – born 3 Sept 1878 Tregony
SHORT A.	Alexander
SNELL T.	Theodore – born 5 March 1889 Tregony
SPEAR J.	Joseph – born 28 June 1890 Gorran
SPEAR W.	William – born 6 May 1886
TOMS H.	Harry – born about 1896
TONKIN J.	-
TOWSEY J.H.	John Headley – born 6 Sept 1890 Tregony
TREGUNNA F.G.	Frederick George
TRUSCOTT C.J.	Cyril John – born 10 July 1891 Tregony
VINCENT H.	Harry – born 16 May 1895 Cuby
WHEELER F.W.	Frederick Walter – born 14 April 1896
WILLIAMS R.J.	-
WILLING C.A.	Clarence Arthur – born 2 Feb 1899 Lanreath

Appendix C

Servicemen Killed in the Second World War

1 DOVE   **Gilbert Henry**

Petty Officer, D/JX 134624 Royal Navy – was killed in action on Wednesday the 13th December 1939, whilst serving on the British Cruiser *H.M.S. Exeter* at the Battle of the 'River Plate', just off Montevideo, Uruguay. As result of this engagement, the German Packet Battleship, *Graf Spee,* was destroyed by its own crew, rather than fall into the hands of the British Navy. Gilbert has no known grave. His name is remembered with honour at the Naval Memorial at the Hoe, Plymouth.

Gilbert, born about 1914, was the son of Thomas Harold & Hephzibah Josephine Olive DOVE of Gurney Row, Tregony. Two years later, Gilbert's brother, Harold, was also killed in action.

2 DOVE   **Harold Leslie**

Leading Seaman, D/JX 132676 Royal Navy – was killed in action on Wednesday 10th December 1941, whilst serving on the Battleship, *H.M.S. Prince of Wales*, during an operation against the Japanese attack on Malaya. Both the *Prince of Wales*, and the battle cruiser, *Repulse,* were sunk during this action. There is no known grave but Harold's name is remembered in honour on the Plymouth Naval Memorial.

Harold, who was born about 1912, was the eldest son of Thomas Harold & Hephzibah Josephine Olive DOVE of Gurney Row, Tregony. In December 1939, Harold's only brother, Gilbert had been killed in action on board *H.M.S. Exeter.*

3 MOORE   **Phillip Henry Hugh**

Gunner, No. 14567732, of the 53rd (The Worcestershire Yeomanry)

Airlanding Light Regiment, Royal Artillery, (part of the 6th Airborne Div) was killed in action on Saturday 24th March 1945 at the crossing of the Rhine at Wesel. He was buried at the Reichswald Forest War Cemetery at Kleve, Nordrhein-Westfalen, Germany. (Grave Ref – joint grave 41.E.10-11.)

Hugh, as he was known, was born about 1923. He was the son of Henry & Mary Matilda MOORE. Mr MOORE (senior) had been the headmaster of the Tregony Council School since 1922 and Hugh had spent all of his life at Tregony.

4 NILE   John

Leading Steward, D/L 1249 of the Royal Navy, was killed on Sunday 17th September 1939, when his ship, the aircraft-carrier, *H.M.S. Courageous* was sunk in the English Channel whilst on convoy escort duty. A German submarine, *U.29*, torpedoed the carrier and 518 men of the 1200 crew were lost. John has no known grave but his name is remembered with honour on the Naval Memorial on the Hoe at Plymouth.

Royal Cornwall Gazette dated 27th Sept 1939 – "Mr J. NILE, aged 49 years, who lost his life when *H.M.S. Courageous* was sunk, had been a postman at Tregoney for eight years. A native of Plymouth, he served through the last war, retired from the Navy nine years ago and went to live at Tregoney. He leaves a widow and two sons."

'Jack', as he was known, was born about 1889. He was the husband of Mrs Mabel Ann NILE of Tregony.

5 POLLARD   Sydney Charles

Private, No. 4950849 of the 7th (Airborne) Battalion; King's Own Scottish Borderers, was killed in action at Arnhem, Holland on Sunday 24th September 1944. He was buried at the Arnhem Oosterbeek War Cemetery at Gelderland, Netherlands (Grave Ref – 22.B.4).

Royal Cornwall Gazette dated 25th October 1944 – "Mrs POLLARD of Tregoney has been officially informed that her husband, Pte S.C. POLLARD, who was with the airborne force at Arnhem, has been reported missing."

'Pop' POLLARD, as he was known, was aged 24 years and was

the husband of Mrs Vera Isabel POLLARD (neé NICHOLLS) of Tregony. His parents were James Henry & Ellen POLLARD.

6 ROBY Thomas

Stoker 1st Class, D/KX 93877 of the Royal Navy died at sea on board the Aircraft Carrier, *H.M.S. Courageous* on Sunday 17th September 1939 when it was torpedoed and sunk by the German U-Boat, *U.29*, in the English Channel. He has no known grave but is remembered with honour on the Naval Memorial on the Hoe at Plymouth.

Although Thomas was not a native of Tregony at the time of his death, his widowed mother, Sarah ROBY, had come to live in Tregony during the War. She later married a Tregonian, Mr Arthur NICHOLLS. Thomas was aged 21 when he died.

7 SMALE Reginald George

Sergeant, No. 944649 of the 118th Field Regiment, Royal, aged 25 years, on Tuesday 12th September 1944 whilst a prisoner of the Japanese. He has no known grave but his name is remembered with honour on the Singapore Memorial in the Kranli War Cemetery.

An Article from the *Tregoney Happenings* 1st May 1946 – "Mrs SMALE, daughter of Mrs Hannah TOWSEY has removed from London to Tregoney to live with and look after her aged mother and her brother. We regret to say her only son Reggie is again reported missing. He was taking part in the war in the Far East, and was reported missing, but later his mother was informed that he was a prisoner in Japanese hands. He was in the ill-fated Japanese ship that was sunk (by American aircraft) whilst conveying prisoners from one part of Japanese-held territory to another and is again amongst the missing. Much sympathy is expressed with his mother and other relatives at Tregoney." [Many other British prisoners were also killed in the same incident.]

Reggie SMALE left a wife, Vera Florence SMALE of Kentish Town, London. A Londoner, he was the son of Mrs Nora SMALE who was a 'Tregony' TOWSEY before she married. After the death of her husband, Nora with Reggie returned to Tregony. He later went back to London where he married. He became a Detective Constable in the Metropolitan Police.

Sources & References

Books

'The Jubilee of County Councils' (Cornwall edition) published by Evans Brothers Ltd, London, 1939.

The Story of Tregony Village Primary School' by the Tregony W.I. 1976 (local distribution).

'Veryan & The Roseland' by Christine Hawkridge, 1967.

Maps

1789 Bassett's Map of Tregony Borough – CRO (DDJ1516).

1828 Tregony Borough – CRO (X829/2).

Tregony Tithe Map 1841 – CRO (TM/44)

1880 Ordnance Survey 24 inch Map.

1907 Ordnance Survey 24 inch Map.

1914 Proposed St Just Railway link & Station at Tregony – CRO (AD/28).

Documents

Bake House in Pig Street, Tregony – Abstract of Deed 1829 – CRO (AD317).

Bible Christian Chapel Account Book – Tregony 1898–1930. (Copy with author).

Bible Christian Chapel Deeds – Mr Alan Grose.

Bill Heading, Thomson Brothers of Tregony 1890s – CRO (AD591/3).

Boscawen Charity (Almshouses), Minute Book 1860-1932– CRO (X982/1-2).

Congregational Chapel, Tregony, notes of Centenary Address 1924 (copy with author).

County Primary School, Tregony, Centenary Souvenir Programme, 1978 (copy with owner).

Cornelly Parish Church History Booklet 1973 (copy with author).

Cuby Parish Church Guide Book 1960 (copy with the author).

Election Advert 1919 Truro RDC, Rev King – CRO (P/44/2.1B).

Harrod's Trade Directory 1878. (The Cornwall Centre, Redruth).

Hart Family unpublished writings on the family, (copy with author).

Kelly's Directories, 1883, 1889, 1902 & 1910.

Letter from W.T. Barnicoat in USA, 1930s (copy with author).

Letter from C.W. Ford in USA, 1920s (copy with author).

Methodist Chapel Histoy, Tregony. The Shaw Methodist Collection – The Courtney Library.

Parsons, Mr K.O. Copy notes on Tregony local history (copy with author).

South Powder Petty Sessions' Court Registers – CRO (AD81/81/25-27).

St James's Oddfellows' Enrolments Registers – CRO (DDX 594/32-59).

Tregony Board School Log Books – CRO (SR/TREG/1-4).

Tregony Market House Conveyance 1857 [copy with the author].

Will of Robert Luke of Tregony, 1836 – CRO (AP/L/2364).

Copies Film & Photographs

Census Returns Tregony Area 1841-1901 (The Cornwall Centre, Redruth).

Non-conformist Religious Census for Tregony 1851 – CRO (FS/2/94/1).

Building Tregony Bridge 1893 – 2 photos – CRO (X230/57/3/156 & 158).

Opening of Public Road Trewarthenick 1921 – Photo – (CRO (AD545/2).

Tregony Square, photos by G. Ellis 1950, No. C.2621 & C2622 (CC Redruth).

Newspapers

Royal Cornwall Gazette 1864 -1930. (Courtney Library & CC Redruth).

West Briton 1900-1920, (CC Redruth).

Other

Commonwealth War Graces Commission Web-site.

Abbreviations

CRO – Cornwall Record Office.

CC – Cornwall Centre.

Conversion Tables

The units of weight, measurement and currency used in this book are of the old imperial, pre-decimalisation type. For the information of future generations who are unfamiliar with this old system, conversion tables are set out below:

Currency
This was based on the units of:

Pounds bank notes (£)
Shillings coins (s. or /-)
Penny or **Pence** coins (d) which also included **half-penny** or **ha'penny** (½d) and **farthing** (¼d).

£1 = 20s = 100p (decimal)
1s = 12d = 5p (decimal)
1d = 2 ha'pennies or 4 farthings = 0.4p (decimal) approx.

Length
The old units were:

Miles
Yards (yds)
Foot or **Feet** (ft or ')
Inches (ins or "]

1 mile = 1760 yds = 1609 metres
1 yd = 3 ft = .9144 metres
1ft = 12" = 30.48 cm
1 ins = 25.4 mm

Area
1 acre = 4047 sq metres

Weight
The original system used:

Tons
Hundredweights (cwt)
Quarters (qrts)
Stones (st)
Pounds (lbs)
Ounces (ozs)

1 ton = 20 cwt = 1.016 tonnes
1 cwt = 4 qrts = 50.8 kgs
1 qrt = 2st = 12.70 kgs
1 st = 14 lbs = 6.35 kgs
1 lb = 16 ozs = 0.453 kg
1 oz = 28.349 gms.

Liquid Measure
Imperial measures used:

Gallons (gal)
Quarts
Pints (pts)
Gills

1 gal = 4 quarts = 4.546 litres
1 quart = 2 pints = 1.1365 litres
1 pint = 4 gills = .5682 litres

PEOPLE - Name Index

General Index

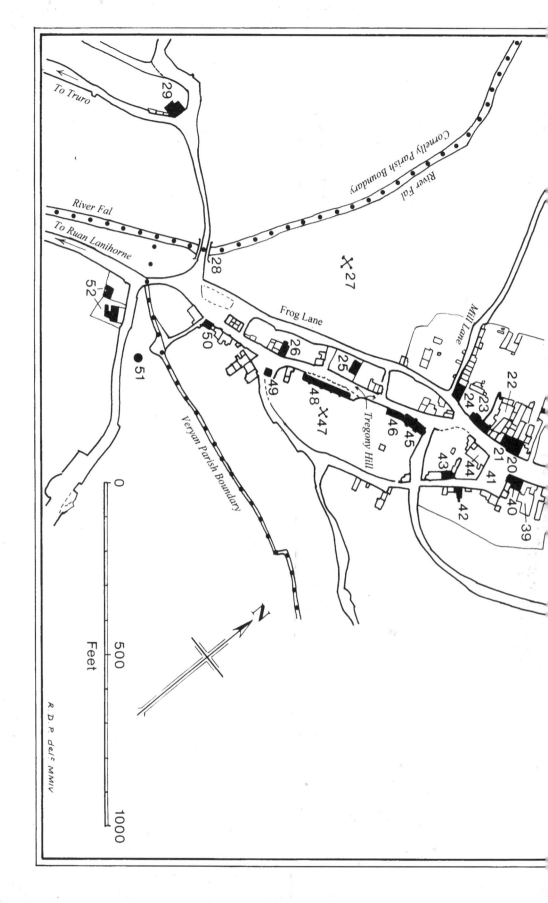

To Truro

29

Cornelly Parish Boundary

River Fal

River Fal

To Ruan Lanihorne

28

×27

52×

Frog Lane

50

●51

26

25

Mill Lane

Tregony Hill

49

48 ×47

46

45

22

24 23

Veryan Parish Boundary

43

44
21
20
41

42

40

39

0

500

Feet

1000

N

R. D. P. delt MMIV